CW00732132

WEATHER WATCHER'S 3-YEAR LOG BOOK

CONTENTS

THE ROYAL METEOROLOGICAL SOCIETY

The Royal Meteorological Society plays a key role as the custodian of both the science and the profession of meteorology in the UK and has an important role to play internationally as one of the world's largest meteorological societies. The Society is owned by its membership, but exists for the benefit of all.

The Society's mission is to promote meteorology as a science, profession and interest and has a wide remit that looks to support people's understanding, interest and enthusiasm in meteorology, whether they are research scientists, amateur meteorologists, practitioners, or members of the general public. It goes further, supporting the development of high-quality science, the next generation of scientists, professional development of individuals, accrediting further and higher education courses, informing policy and supporting learning in weather and climate through education and outreach activities.

INTRODUCTION

Congratulations on being the proud owner of a *Weather Watcher's 3-Year Log Book*. This book provides you with an opportunity to capture information about the weather on a daily basis so you can follow in the footsteps of others who share your passion and interest in the weather. As you start to collect information you can begin to see changes and trends on a daily, monthly, seasonal and annual basis. You'll soon collate a personal record that describes the climate where you live. You may decide to share this information with others using a number of different websites detailed at the end of the book in the 'To Find Out More' section.

The book not only provides an elegant way of capturing information about the weather, it also answers questions like 'How do clouds form?' and describes the different weather phenomena that you may observe, such as lightning, snow and fog. Combined with beautiful illustrations by the artist Elissa Nesheim, this log book is something you will treasure for many years.

I've been fascinated by the weather from an early age and used to keep my own weather records as a teenager growing up in Yorkshire. I'd use this information, along with a synoptic weather chart from the local newspaper, to try and forecast the weather. The weather on top of the Pennines was always that bit more extreme – there were all those winter mornings waking up to find snow so deep you needed to dig your way out of the house, which I loved. And the horizontal rain and gale force winds as I walked to school, meaning I arrived for class with my front half soaking and the rest of me bone dry. These I loved somewhat less, but they always left me wondering how and why.
A career in meteorology was an obvious choice before I'd even left school and this passion has never left me. I still love seeing a covering of snow. I still get excited when I hear the thunder and see the lightning, experiencing the weather at its angriest.

When you tell people you're a meteorologist you soon realise everyone has an interest. They either ask you for a forecast or blame you for the poor weather. Sometimes they will tell you a weather anecdote of their own. Often they will admit to their own fascination as if it's been a guilty secret for years. I hope you enjoy collating your own weather log book and, who knows, it may inspire some meteorologists for the future.

Professor Liz Bentley
Chief Executive of the Royal Meteorological Society

HOW TO USE THIS BOOK

Recording and making notes on the weather can be a fascinating occupation. Yesterday's weather is probably not the same as the weather today. The changes you have noticed can be logged in this book and as the days go by you will build up a record of not just the weather but how it changes over time – what meteorologists call the climate.

You can use special weather instruments to take measurements. Alternatively, you can make your own or just use your eyes and ears. If you don't have any special equipment it would be useful if you have an outdoors thermometer to put on a shady side of a building where direct sunlight will not reach it, as well as close sight of a weather vane or even a tree for showing wind direction.

There are four images repeated on the weekly record pages.
These stand for:

Temperature

Cloud cover

Rain

Wind direction

You can use the symbols below to fill out the log. These are the kind of symbols you would see on a meteorologist's weather chart.

Temperature   °C or Kelvin, K (0°C is equivalent to approx 273K)

Rain   • (light) •• (medium) ••• (heavy)

Cloud cover   ○ (clear) ◑ (partly 4/8 covered)
                   ● (sky covered) ⊗ (sky obscured e.g. by fog)

Wind direction   ⟶ (wind comes FROM direction of arrow)

The log book divides records up into days and weeks.

Choose a time to go outside and observe the weather. Try to keep to the same time each day. First thing in the morning between 8 and 9 a.m. is a good time, or perhaps a regular lunchtime slot. You can record the kind of weather by using the symbols opposite, or by describing it or even by drawing it.

In the section marked 'Observations', you can write a comment about the weather on a daily basis. On the right is an example of a section we have filled out.

JANUARY

YEAR:

OBSERVATIONS

1 Mild but with light drizzle Time:	12°C	•	◑	←
2 Rained most of the day Time:	11°C	••	●	←
3 Time:	9°C		◕	↖
4 Cooler with stronger winds Time:	8°C		○	↖
5 Very clear rainbow Time:	10°C	•	◑	→
6 Time:	9°C		◑	↘
7 Time:	10°C	•	◕	→
WEEKLY SUMMARY AND AVERAGES:	10°C	•	◑	

MEASURING THE WEATHER

Making observations is the essential basis of recording the weather. Visual observations are useful and can be combined with measurements using simple measuring instruments, which can be made with the minimum of cost. The following suggestions will allow you to take basic but effective weather records. In the main we have referred to 'traditional' instruments, but there is now a wide range of digital instruments available at competitive prices. Don't worry too much about the accuracy of the instrument, it won't be up to Met Office standards, but will usually be fine for looking at differences from day to day, through the seasons and from year to year.

TEMPERATURE
If you are going to measure only one weather 'element', then the temperature of the air is a good choice.

There are different thermometers available, including digital temperature sensors, but the usual liquid-in-glass type is preferable. In this type the liquid (usually spirit) in the bulb expands and rises up a capillary tube to a height that depends upon the temperature, which can be read off a graduated scale alongside.

The scale should be as open and clear as possible, with graduations every whole degree and labels at least every ten degrees. The temperature scale used in most countries is now degrees Celsius, although Fahrenheit is still found on some thermometers on sale in places such as garden centres.

Placing the thermometer
Place the thermometer out of direct sunlight, so that it reads the temperature of the air, not the temperature to which it has itself been heated by the sun. If you are really serious about improving accuracy it helps if the thermometer can be in some sort of simple screen – a white-painted box with no base, for instance, or even a short section of white PVC drainpipe, open at both ends.

If making a screen is too difficult, then hanging the thermometer on a north-facing wall is the best alternative. The daily maximum temperature usually occurs at about 14:00 (use the 24-hour clock for recording all measurements).

Maximum and minimum thermometer
If you want to record true daily temperature extremes, then a maximum and minimum (max-min) thermometer is needed. This will also, of course, serve as an ordinary thermometer.

The recommended type of thermometer for reading max/min temperatures is a liquid-in-glass type – called a Six's thermometer. The max/min thermometer should be exposed as for the ordinary thermometer. Normally the max/min thermometer is reset in the evening of each day.

RAINFALL

Just about any container that is the same width all the way down and with a flat bottom can be used to collect rainfall. The amount of rain collected can be measured simply by dipping something into the water and measuring the depth in millimetres. Whilst this is very simple (and free), there is one disadvantage that can be overcome by using a slightly more sophisticated design. Depths of a millimetre or two are difficult to measure, so by using a water storage and measuring container with a collecting funnel of larger diameter, the depth of water collected will be correspondingly increased and easier to measure. Simple rain-gauges of this type are available at garden centres, online or you can make one.
Rain-gauges should be placed in the open and, if possible, preferably more than 5m (16 ft) from any buildings.
For useful information about the history of rain-gauges and tips on how to make your own rain-gauge go to the Royal Meteorological Society's website (www.rmets.org).

SNOWFALL

In many parts of Britain, especially the south, there are very few days when the snow lies more than a few millimetres deep. When it does, though, it is a big talking point. The depth can be measured quite easily with a simple ruler (don't forget to account for the 'dead space' on the end, of course), preferably in a place where the snow has not drifted.

PRESSURE

Pressure can be measured in millibars with a simple barometer. Atmospheric pressure is related to the weight of the column of air above your barometer, so this depends on how high your house is above sea-level. Lifting up the barometer by about 8m (26ft) gives a decrease of about 1 millibar (mbar). Changes in pressure are associated with different types of weather. You can calibrate your barometer and adjust it to sea-level pressure at the same time, by ringing up the Met Office. Just after midday is the best time, preferably on a clear and calm day when the pressure will not be changing rapidly or varying from place to place. There are also websites which show real-time data and give pressure within the last hour. An example is www.bbc.co.uk/weather, just enter your postcode to get a current observation of the weather near you, including the pressure.

WIND SPEED AND DIRECTION

The wind direction is expressed in terms of the direction from which the wind blows. It can be estimated relatively easily by looking at trees or at flags or weather vanes. Weather vanes are one of the oldest of all weather instruments, working by swinging around in the wind to show which direction it is blowing from. Traditionally, weather vanes had a religious importance and appeared in the form of weathercocks on church roofs as early as the ninth century AD. Weather vanes should be sited as high as possible and they need to be sensitive enough to respond to a light breeze, yet robust enough to withstand strong gales.

If there are trees or other suitable indicators around, wind speed can be estimated using the Beaufort scale (see right). In 1806, Admiral Francis Beaufort promoted a scale of this type for measuring winds at sea by describing their effect on ships and waves. His scale was later adapted for use on land, and the same system is still used today.

SUNSHINE, CLOUD COVER AND VISIBILITY

There are different types of devices available for measuring the amount of sunshine. However, visual observations of cloud are simple to make and record. Some standard observations often made are:

• **Cloud amount** This is the proportion of sky covered by cloud which can be described as: 'clear', 'partly cloudy' (i.e. less than half cloudy), 'mainly cloudy' and 'completely cloudy'. However, the internationally recognized measure of cloud cover is the number of eighths of the sky that is covered in cloud.

• **Cloud type** This can be as simple or as complicated as you want. You can describe clouds with their names (see pages 16–19) or simply describe them as 'high', 'low', 'layer-type', 'bubbly' etc.

In addition to observing the state of the sky, it is also worthwhile recording the visibility. This can be measured by reference to a number of known landmarks at different distances. Three or four landmarks at, for example, 100m (110 yards), 1,000m (1,090 yards), 2km (1.24 miles) and 10km (6.21 miles), will allow the visibility to be described as 'thick fog', 'fog', 'poor visibility' and 'good visibility' respectively.

BEAUFORT WIND SCALE FOR LAND AREAS

- Make your observations in an open location
- Remember the scale is only an estimate of wind speed
- Enter 'calm' if there is no wind

Wind Force	Description	Speed		Specifications
		km/h	knots	
0	Calm	0	0	Smoke rises vertically
1	Light Air	1–5	1–3	Direction shown by smoke drift but not by wind vanes
2	Light Breeze	6–11	4–6	Wind felt on face; leaves rustle; wind vane moved by wind
3	Gentle Breeze	12–19	7–10	Leaves, small twigs in constant motion; light flags extended
4	Moderate Breeze	20–28	11–16	Raises dust and loose paper; small branches moved
5	Fresh Breeze	29–38	17–21	Small trees in leaf begin to sway; crested wavelets form on inland waters
6	Strong Breeze	39–49	22–27	Large branches in motion; whistling heard in telegraph wires; umbrellas used with difficulty
7	Near Gale	50–61	28–33	Whole trees in motion; inconvenience felt when walking against the wind
8	Gale	62–74	34–40	Twigs break off trees; generally impedes progress
9	Strong Gale	75–88	41–47	Slight structural damage (chimney pots and slates removed)
10	Storm	89–102	48–55	Seldom experienced inland; trees uprooted; considerable structural damage
11	Violent Storm	103–117	56–63	Very rarely experienced; accompanied by widespread damage
12	Hurricane	118+	64+	Devastation
1 knot = 0.514 metres per second = 1.152 miles per hour (mph) = 1.853 kilometres per hour (km/h)				

A HEAD IN THE CLOUDS – LUKE HOWARD

Luke Howard (1772–1864) was a British meteorologist with broad interests in science. His legacy to science is a classification system for clouds. In his late twenties he wrote the Essay on the Modification of Clouds, which was published in 1802. He named the three principal categories of clouds – cumulus, stratus, and cirrus, as well as a series of intermediate descriptions, such as cirrostratus and stratocumulus, in order to account for clouds changing into different types. His cloud classifications were based upon the altitude and visual appearance of the cloud.

Here are some of Luke Howard's definitions of clouds which are used to this day.
Cumulus (Latin for 'heap') – Convex or conical heaps, increasing upward from a horizontal base.
Stratus (Latin for 'spread' or 'sheet') – Widely extended horizontal sheets/layers.
Cirrus (Latin for 'curl') – Fibrous or hair-like and could also be described as 'wispy'.
Nimbus (Latin for 'rainy cloud') – Rain-bearing (usually appear dark grey).

Not all clouds bring rain – some are signs of fine weather, which explains why the fourth type is needed. 'Nimbus' can be added to the beginning or end of a cloud type, e.g., cumulonimbus or nimbostratus.

In all there are ten main categories of cloud generally used nowadays with names made up from the four Latin words introduced by Luke Howard.
These can be broadly classified as follows:
High-level clouds: Cirrus, Cirrostratus and Cirrocumulus
Mid-level clouds: Altostratus and Altocumulus
Low-level clouds: Stratus, Stratocumulus and Nimbostratus
Clouds with vertical development: Cumulus and Cumulonimbus

HOW CLOUDS ARE FORMED

Everywhere in the world, the air in our atmosphere contains an invisible gas called water vapour. This is water that has evaporated, mostly from the oceans, but also from lakes, soils and vegetation. The process of rain falling and then evaporating back into the atmosphere is a simple example of what is called the 'water cycle'. Clouds and fog are made of water droplets which form when water vapour condenses back from a gas to a liquid. The typical size of one water droplet is about one hundredth of a millimetre and there are about 100 droplets in each cubic centimetre (0.06 cubic inches) of cloud.

Clouds are very common and cover on average around 50% of the Earth at any given time, helping to keep the Earth's temperature within a habitable range. There are three main types of cloud which were described on the previous page.

Cirrus – Wispy clouds (see page 16) which occur high in the sky (above 6,000m/20,000ft) where it is very cold. They are made of tiny ice crystals rather than water droplets.

Cumulus – Fluffy-looking cumulus clouds (see page 18) are perhaps the most familiar clouds and look like heaps of cotton wool or large cauliflowers. Cumulus clouds are low-level clouds which are composed of tiny water droplets.

Stratus – Low-level blankets of cloud (see page 19) which appear as a grey, shapeless layer of cloud extending in all directions across the sky. They are usually only about 1km (0.62 miles) thick, but can be as much as 1,000km (621 miles) wide.

There are two main ways in which clouds can form: through the buoyancy or forced lifting of air.

CLOUDS FORMED BY BUOYANT WARM AIR

On a sunny day the sun's rays heat the ground and consequently the air in contact with the ground is warmed. The warmer air is less dense than the cooler air above it, and so it rises naturally, in buoyant up-currents called thermals. These are what glider pilots rely on to keep them airborne. As the air in a thermal rises, it cools. The water vapour in the thermal condenses into water droplets and a cloud forms. The height at which the cloud starts to form depends on the amount of water vapour in the air; this height is called the condensation level. You will have seen this quite often when looking up at a cloudy sky and seeing that clouds have a relatively flat base all at the same level. Low-level clouds such as cumulus clouds have a very well-defined base (see page 18). If thermals are very strong then cumulus clouds grow upwards to form dark, towering, cumulonimbus clouds (see page 19). We often get heavy rain showers from these clouds and also thunder and lightning, and sometimes hail. The tops of the clouds may be as high as 10km (6.21 miles) in the UK, but climb to much greater heights in tropical regions.

CLOUDS FORMED WHEN AIR IS FORCED TO RISE

Air can be forced to rise for a number of reasons. Firstly, when air meets a range of mountains or hills it has to rise to get over them. As it rises, the air cools and condensation occurs. The second process is where air cools and condenses as a result of frontal uplift. Fronts are boundaries between air masses of different temperature and humidity. When these air masses meet they do not readily mix. Instead they remain separate, with the cooler and denser air mass undercutting the warmer less dense air mass. This process leads to the upward movement of the warm air. As it rises, the warm air cools, resulting in condensation and therefore cloud formation. However, unlike the cumulus clouds formed when air rises because it is buoyant, clouds in air being forced to rise will often spread out to form a flat featureless layer of stratus cloud. Sometimes light rain, often referred to as drizzle, forms in stratus clouds. Stratus can also break up into smaller pieces to form a mix of stratus and cumulus which is known as stratocumulus. To find out how to identify the different cloud types see pages 16–19. Stratus clouds can also form over the sea, for example when warm moist air from the south is cooled by contact with the cold sea as it moves northwards. The clouds can then blow inland near the coast.

CONDENSATION TRAILS

Known as contrails, these clouds form from the water vapour emitted from aircraft engines. Exhaust gases cool rapidly mainly due to the mixing of these hot moist gases with their cold surroundings. If the air is sufficiently cold, the water droplets freeze into ice and, if the humidity is high enough, can sometimes spread sufficiently to form extensive patches of cirrus clouds which are considered an important impact of aviation on climate.

WHY THERE ARE SOMETIMES NO CLOUDS

Sometimes, even on warm sunny afternoons, there are no clouds. The most likely reason for this is that we are under the influence of an area of air where atmospheric pressure is high – an anticyclone. Air in an anticyclone is sinking slowly – typically a few metres every hour.
The air which is sinking in an anticyclone can become warmer than the air below it, and thus creates what is called an inversion of the temperature. The inversion forms a 'lid' and so stops air rising from the surface. If the height of the inversion is below the condensation level then the rising air cannot reach high enough for the water vapour to condense and so no clouds form.

CLOUDS AND FORECASTING THE WEATHER

Clouds can help us forecast the weather locally. If the amount of cumulus cloud increases rapidly during the morning, then it would be wise to take an umbrella as towering cumulonimbus may develop in the afternoon and give local showers. On the other hand, if thin high cirrus cloud thickens into altostratus then a warm front may be approaching, and widespread rain from nimbostratus may follow.

HOW TO IDENTIFY CLOUDS

ALTITUDE OF CLOUD BASE	CLOUD TYPE	SHAPE AND APPEARANCE	
HIGH Above 6,000m (20,000ft)	Cirrus (Ci)	White, delicate, silky and fibrous (hair-like) in appearance. Forms into patches or narrow bands.	
HIGH Above 6,000m (20,000ft)	Cirrus uncinus (Ci unc)	White, delicate, fibrous strands, comma- or hook-shaped.	
HIGH Above 6,000m (20,000ft)	Cirrostratus (Cs)	A thin, transparent, white veil through which the sun is clearly visible and casting shadows. A halo around the sun is sometimes visible. A halo can sometimes be seen around the moon, especially a full moon.	
HIGH Above 6,000m (20,000ft)	Cirrocumulus (Cc)	A thin white patch, sheet or layer of cloud, which may be dappled or rippled in appearance.	

ALTITUDE OF CLOUD BASE	CLOUD TYPE	SHAPE AND APPEARANCE	
HIGH Above 6,000m (20,000ft)	Aircraft contrails	Caused by the passage of aircraft through the atmosphere. Thin and white cirrus clouds which follow a single linear path. Often short-lived, although sometimes very persistent.	
MEDIUM 2,000–6,000m (6,500–20,000ft)	Altostratus (As)	A greyish sheet/layer, fibrous or uniform in appearance. Thin enough in parts to reveal the sun, as if viewed through ground glass. No halo.	
MEDIUM 2,000–6,000m (6,500–20,000ft)	Altocumulus lenticularis (Ac len)	White or grey broken clouds, in lens or almond shapes, usually with clear outlines. Formed by air movement over a topographic barrier.	
MEDIUM 2,000–6,000m (6,500–20,000ft)	Altocumulus castellanus (Ac cas)	White or grey broken, cumulus-like clouds, with upper part appearing as a castle turret. Sometimes the clouds are arranged in lines.	

ALTITUDE OF CLOUD BASE	CLOUD TYPE	SHAPE AND APPEARANCE	
MEDIUM 2,000–6,000m (6,500–20,000ft)	Altocumulus undulatus (Ac und)	White or grey patches or sheets/layers of cloud with an undulating appearance.	
MEDIUM 2,000–6,000m (6,500–20,000ft)	Altocumulus (other types) (Ac)	White or grey clumps, patches or sheets/layers of cloud. Can occur in variable shapes and textures.	
LOW Below 2,000m (6,500ft)	Cumulus (Cu)	Brilliant white to grey, dense, detached clouds. Forms clumped/heaped (cauliflower) shapes, usually with sharp outlines.	
LOW Below 2,000m (6,500ft)	Stratocumulus (Sc)	Grey to whitish layer of cloud which usually forms rounded masses or rolls.	

ALTITUDE OF CLOUD BASE	CLOUD TYPE	SHAPE AND APPEARANCE	
LOW Below 2,000m (6,500ft)	Stratus (St)	Grey, featureless sheet/layer of cloud with uniform base. Often associated with drizzle or snow grains.	
LOW Below 2,000m (6,500ft)	Fractostratus (St fra)	Grey sheet/layer of cloud, which has an irregular ragged/torn/ shredded appearance.	
LOW with precipitation	Cumulonimbus (Cb)	Huge, towering cloud with dark base and white sides. Associated with heavy precipitation, thunderstorms and hail. Often has an anvil-shaped top.	
LOW with precipitation	Nimbostratus (Ns)	Dark grey, featureless, thick layer of cloud. Associated with prolonged precipitation.	

WEATHER EXTREMES

Sunniest place
Yuma, Arizona, is one of the sunniest places in the world, experiencing an average of 4,055 hours of sunshine (out of a possible 4,456 hours) per year.

Wettest place
There are a few contenders for the wettest place in the world. The weather station on Mount Wai'ale'ale, Kauai, one of the Hawaiian islands, records on average 11,640mm (460in) rain per year. Rain falls on between 335 and 360 days per year. Cherrapunji in north-east India regularly gets over 10,000mm (394in) per year. Its near neighbour Mawsynram, has an average annual rainfall of 11,872mm (467in).

Most rainfall in one minute
The most intense rainfall ever recorded was on the 4 July 1956 in Unionville, Maryland, where 31.2mm (1.23in) fell in one minute.

Warmest year
The warmest year on record was 2016 with a global average temperature of 14.8°C (59°F).

Highest temperature in the UK
The highest temperature in the UK is 38.5°C (101°F) reached in Brogdale, near Faversham, Kent on 10 August 2003.

Lowest temperature in the UK
The lowest temperature in the UK ever reached is -27.2°C (-17°F) at two locations: Braemar, Grampian on 11 February 1895 and 10 January 1982 and Altnaharra, Highland on 30 December 1995.

Coldest place
The lowest outdoor temperature ever recorded is -89.2°C (-129°F) registered at the Vostok Scientific Station in Antarctica on 21 July 1983.

Hottest place
On 10 July 1913 a record-breaking temperature of 56.7°C (134°F) was recorded at Furnace Creek, California.

Driest place
The driest place in the world is Arica in Chile with an annual average precipitation of 0.762mm (0.03in).

Strongest wind gust
The fastest wind speed not related to tornadoes ever recorded was during the passage of Tropical Cyclone Olivia on 10 April 1996: an automatic weather station on Barrow Island, Australia, registered a maximum wind gust of 407km/h (253mph).

Longest-lasting rainbow
A rainbow usually only lasts a few minutes. However, on 14 March 1994, a rainbow was visible over Wetherby, West Yorkshire for six hours from 9 am to 3 pm.

Tallest cloud
The cumulonimbus cloud has been seen to reach a height of nearly 20,000 metres (65,620ft) in the tropics – twice as high as Mt Everest.

Heaviest snowfall
The heaviest recorded 24-hour snowfall was 190cm (75in) which occurred at Silver Lake, Colorado, USA on 14–15 April 1921.

Thickest ice sheet
The east Antarctic ice sheet is the single largest piece of ice on Earth and at some regions it is almost 4.8km (2.98m) thick. The thickest part of ice ever measured was 320km (199m) inland of Wilkes Land in Antarctica.

MORNING HAS BROKEN: DEW AND FROST

○ Dew consists of innumerable tiny droplets of water, which are deposited on the leaves of plants and other objects such as car windscreens overnight. Just as a glass of cold water will cool the air in contact with it enough to form condensation, water vapour in the air can condense onto any cold surface.

○ A clear night and still air are ideal conditions for a dewy morning.

○ The heaviest dews occur when moist warm air moves in over a colder surface as sometimes happens when the weather suddenly changes after a cold spell.

○ Dew is an essential source of moisture for plant and animal life where there is little rainfall.

○ Hoar frost (commonly just called frost) is the frozen equivalent of dew. It forms on clear, calm nights when the air next to the ground has cooled sufficiently for condensation to occur and the temperature near the ground has fallen below 0°C (32°F). The frost consists of soft white ice crystals in the form of needles, scales, feathers or fans which appear on grass, bushes, tree roots and other surfaces.

○ Some sheltered and low-lying areas are particularly susceptible to frost both in terms of frequency and severity. These areas are known as frost hollows.

JANUARY

YEAR:

OBSERVATIONS

1 Time:				
2 Time:				
3 Time:				
4 Time:				
5 Time:				
6 Time:				
7 Time:				
WEEKLY SUMMARY AND AVERAGES:				

YEAR:

OBSERVATIONS

1 Time:
2 Time:
3 Time:
4 Time:
5 Time:
6 Time:
7 Time:
WEEKLY SUMMARY AND AVERAGES:

YEAR:

OBSERVATIONS

1 Time:				
2 Time:				
3 Time:				
4 Time:				
5 Time:				
6 Time:				
7 Time:				
WEEKLY SUMMARY AND AVERAGES:				

JANUARY

OBSERVATIONS

YEAR:

OBSERVATIONS

8 Time:				
9 Time:				
10 Time:				
11 Time:				
12 Time:				
13 Time:				
14 Time:				
WEEKLY SUMMARY AND AVERAGES:				

8 Time:
9 Time:
10 Time:
11 Time:
12 Time:
13 Time:
14 Time:
WEEKLY SUMMARY AND AVERAGES:

OBSERVATIONS

8 Time:				
9 Time:				
10 Time:				
11 Time:				
12 Time:				
13 Time:				
14 Time:				
WEEKLY SUMMARY AND AVERAGES:				

JANUARY

OBSERVATIONS

YEAR:

OBSERVATIONS

15 Time:				
16 Time:				
17 Time:				
18 Time:				
19 Time:				
20 Time:				
21 Time:				
WEEKLY SUMMARY AND AVERAGES:				

15 Time:				
16 Time:				
17 Time:				
18 Time:				
19 Time:				
20 Time:				
21 Time:				
WEEKLY SUMMARY AND AVERAGES:				

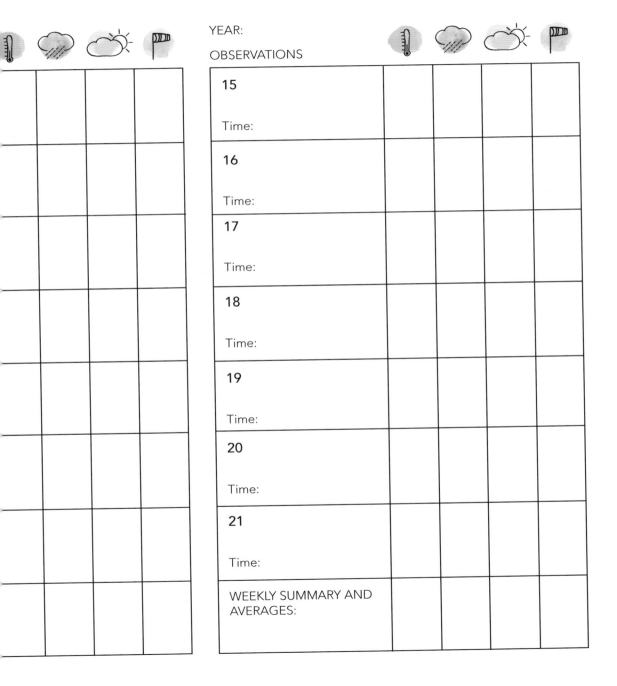

YEAR:

OBSERVATIONS

					15 Time:				
					16 Time:				
					17 Time:				
					18 Time:				
					19 Time:				
					20 Time:				
					21 Time:				
					WEEKLY SUMMARY AND AVERAGES:				

JANUARY

OBSERVATIONS

22				
Time:				
23				
Time:				
24				
Time:				
25				
Time:				
26				
Time:				
27				
Time:				
28				
Time:				
WEEKLY SUMMARY AND AVERAGES:				

YEAR:

OBSERVATIONS

22	
Time:	
23	
Time:	
24	
Time:	
25	
Time:	
26	
Time:	
27	
Time:	
28	
Time:	
WEEKLY SUMMARY AND AVERAGES:	

OBSERVATIONS

				22				
				Time:				
				23				
				Time:				
				24				
				Time:				
				25				
				Time:				
				26				
				Time:				
				27				
				Time:				
				28				
				Time:				
				WEEKLY SUMMARY AND AVERAGES:				

BOLT OUT OF THE BLUE: LIGHTNING

o   Lightning is essentially a gigantic electrical spark that results from
    millions of volts of natural electricity.

o   Lightning causes thunder and can sometimes cause wildfires and
    surges in electric power lines.

o   Lightning and thunder happen at the same time but you always
    see the lightning before you hear the thunder. This is because light
    travels much faster than sound.

o   The most thundery place on Earth is Java, where thunderstorms
    occur on more than 200 days per year.

o   Lightning can travel at a speed of 160,000km/h (100,000mph) and
    temperatures within lightning can reach 28,000°C (50,000°F).

o   Thunder is an explosion caused by the rapid heating and
    expansion of the air within a lightning strike.

o   The most common type of lightning occurs between clouds, but is
    cloud-to-ground lightning which is a threat to life and property.

JANUARY / FEBRUARY

YEAR:

OBSERVATIONS

29 Time:				
30 Time:				
31 Time:				
1 Time:				
2 Time:				
3 Time:				
4 Time:				
WEEKLY SUMMARY AND AVERAGES:				

YEAR:

OBSERVATIONS

29 Time:				
30 Time:				
31 Time:				
1 Time:				
2 Time:				
3 Time:				
4 Time:				
WEEKLY SUMMARY AND AVERAGES:				

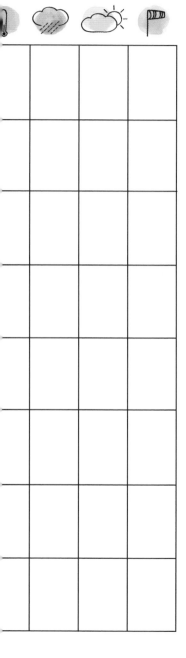

OBSERVATIONS

29 Time:				
30 Time:				
31 Time:				
1 Time:				
2 Time:				
3 Time:				
4 Time:				
WEEKLY SUMMARY AND AVERAGES:				

FEBRUARY

OBSERVATIONS

5 Time:				
6 Time:				
7 Time:				
8 Time:				
9 Time:				
10 Time:				
11 Time:				
WEEKLY SUMMARY AND AVERAGES:				

YEAR:

OBSERVATIONS

5 Time:				
6 Time:				
7 Time:				
8 Time:				
9 Time:				
10 Time:				
11 Time:				
WEEKLY SUMMARY AND AVERAGES:				

OBSERVATIONS

				5 Time:				
				6 Time:				
				7 Time:				
				8 Time:				
				9 Time:				
				10 Time:				
				11 Time:				
				WEEKLY SUMMARY AND AVERAGES:				

FEBRUARY

YEAR:

OBSERVATIONS

YEAR:

OBSERVATIONS

12 Time:				
13 Time:				
14 Time:				
15 Time:				
16 Time:				
17 Time:				
18 Time:				
WEEKLY SUMMARY AND AVERAGES:				

12 Time:				
13 Time:				
14 Time:				
15 Time:				
16 Time:				
17 Time:				
18 Time:				
WEEKLY SUMMARY AND AVERAGES:				

					YEAR:

OBSERVATIONS

				12 Time:				
				13 Time:				
				14 Time:				
				15 Time:				
				16 Time:				
				17 Time:				
				18 Time:				
				WEEKLY SUMMARY AND AVERAGES:				

FEBRUARY

YEAR:

OBSERVATIONS

19 Time:				
20 Time:				
21 Time:				
22 Time:				
23 Time:				
24 Time:				
25 Time:				
WEEKLY SUMMARY AND AVERAGES:				

YEAR:

OBSERVATIONS

19 Time:
20 Time:
21 Time:
22 Time:
23 Time:
24 Time:
25 Time:
WEEKLY SUMMARY AND AVERAGES:

19 Time:				
20 Time:				
21 Time:				
22 Time:				
23 Time:				
24 Time:				
25 Time:				
WEEKLY SUMMARY AND AVERAGES:				

RICHARD OF YORK GAVE BATTLE IN VAIN: RAINBOWS

- The colours of the rainbow always appear in the same order. Red is on the outside, then orange, yellow, green, blue, indigo and violet on the inside. Many people use the phrase 'Richard of York Gave Battle In Vain' to help them remember the colours of the rainbow.

- A rainbow is formed when sunlight is broken up into a spectrum of colours by raindrops or droplets of water of other kinds (spray over waterfalls, for example, or the droplets produced by hose-pipes and car washes). The sun must be behind you and the rain in front to see a rainbow. Consequently, rainbows are often seen when there are showers.

- Rainbows have no end because they are circles (so you will never find a pot of gold at the end of a rainbow!). You can sometimes see the complete circle of a rainbow from an airplane.

- The height of the top of the rainbow depends on the sun's altitude: the lower the sun, the higher the arc.

- The brightness of the colours of a rainbow depends on the size of the water droplets. Large drops give bright colours.

FEBRUARY / MARCH

OBSERVATIONS

26 Time:				
27 Time:				
28 Time:				
29 Time:				
1 Time:				
2 Time:				
3 Time:				
WEEKLY SUMMARY AND AVERAGES:				

YEAR:

OBSERVATIONS

26 Time:				
27 Time:				
28 Time:				
29 Time:				
1 Time:				
2 Time:				
3 Time:				
WEEKLY SUMMARY AND AVERAGES:				

OBSERVATIONS

26 Time:				
27 Time:				
28 Time:				
29 Time:				
1 Time:				
2 Time:				
3 Time:				
WEEKLY SUMMARY AND AVERAGES:				

MARCH

YEAR:

OBSERVATIONS

YEAR:

OBSERVATIONS

4 Time:				
5 Time:				
6 Time:				
7 Time:				
8 Time:				
9 Time:				
10 Time:				
WEEKLY SUMMARY AND AVERAGES:				

4 Time:				
5 Time:				
6 Time:				
7 Time:				
8 Time:				
9 Time:				
10 Time:				
WEEKLY SUMMARY AND AVERAGES:				

OBSERVATIONS

				4 Time:			
				5 Time:			
				6 Time:			
				7 Time:			
				8 Time:			
				9 Time:			
				10 Time:			
				WEEKLY SUMMARY AND AVERAGES:			

MARCH

YEAR:

OBSERVATIONS

11				
Time:				
12				
Time:				
13				
Time:				
14				
Time:				
15				
Time:				
16				
Time:				
17				
Time:				
WEEKLY SUMMARY AND AVERAGES:				

YEAR:

OBSERVATIONS

11
Time:
12
Time:
13
Time:
14
Time:
15
Time:
16
Time:
17
Time:
WEEKLY SUMMARY AND AVERAGES:

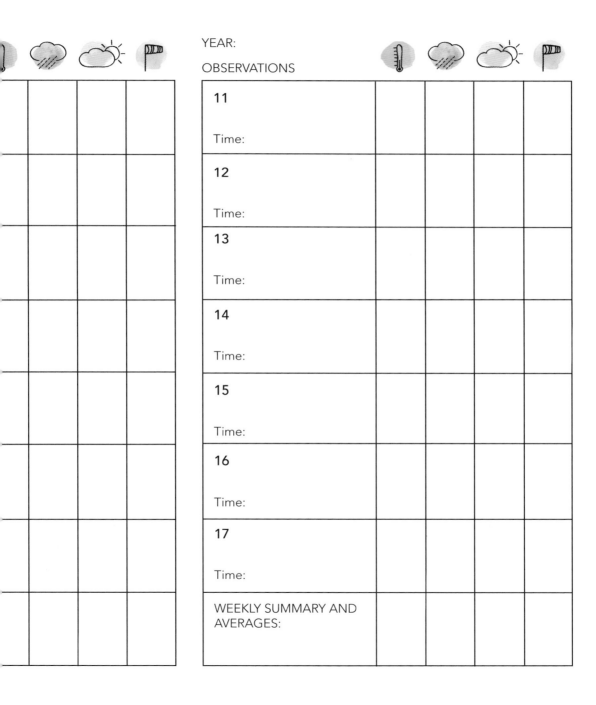

YEAR:

OBSERVATIONS

				11					
				Time:					
				12					
				Time:					
				13					
				Time:					
				14					
				Time:					
				15					
				Time:					
				16					
				Time:					
				17					
				Time:					
				WEEKLY SUMMARY AND AVERAGES:					

MARCH

18 Time:					18 Time:			
19 Time:					19 Time:			
20 Time:					20 Time:			
21 Time:					21 Time:			
22 Time:					22 Time:			
23 Time:					23 Time:			
24 Time:					24 Time:			
WEEKLY SUMMARY AND AVERAGES:					WEEKLY SUMMARY AND AVERAGES:			

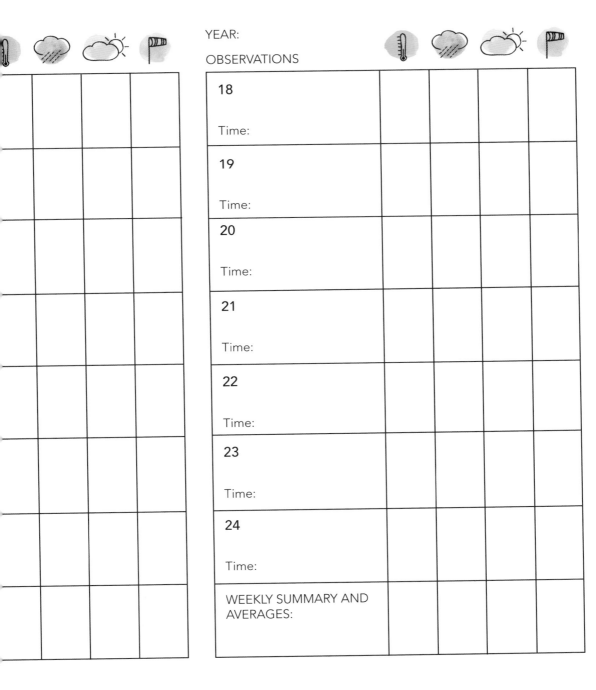

YEAR:

OBSERVATIONS

				18 Time:				
				19 Time:				
				20 Time:				
				21 Time:				
				22 Time:				
				23 Time:				
				24 Time:				
				WEEKLY SUMMARY AND AVERAGES:				

MARCH

25 Time:						**25** Time:				
26 Time:						**26** Time:				
27 Time:						**27** Time:				
28 Time:						**28** Time:				
29 Time:						**29** Time:				
30 Time:						**30** Time:				
31 Time:						**31** Time:				
WEEKLY SUMMARY AND AVERAGES:						WEEKLY SUMMARY AND AVERAGES:				

OBSERVATIONS

					25 Time:				
					26 Time:				
					27 Time:				
					28 Time:				
					29 Time:				
					30 Time:				
					31 Time:				
					WEEKLY SUMMARY AND AVERAGES:				

WATERWORLD: PRECIPITATION

- Any water droplets or ice crystals that are falling towards the ground are known as precipitation.

- Showers (of liquid or solid precipitation) fall from cumulus-type clouds. Intermittent precipitation falls from layer clouds that are of variable thickness but cover all or most of the sky.

- Familiar precipitation includes: Drizzle: droplet size below 0.5mm (0.02in); Rain: droplet size above 0.5mm (0.02in); Snow: clusters of ice crystals; Hail: solid lumps of ice; Sleet: melting snowflakes or a mixture of rain and snow.

- A total of 500,000 tonnes of rain can fall from a single thunderstorm. That's the same as nearly 65,000 London buses!

- The maximum rainfall over 24 hours in the UK was 341.4mm (13.44in) which fell at Honister Pass, Cumbria, between 6pm on 4 December and 6pm on 5 December 2015.

- Because of their resistance to air, fallling raindrops are not tear-shaped, as shown in cartoons, but resemble small buns.

- The heaviest single hailstone recorded weighed about 1kg (2.20lbs). It fell in Bangladesh on 14 April 1986 and the hailstorm was reported to have killed 92 people.

APRIL

YEAR:

OBSERVATIONS

1 Time:				
2 Time:				
3 Time:				
4 Time:				
5 Time:				
6 Time:				
7 Time:				
WEEKLY SUMMARY AND AVERAGES:				

YEAR:

OBSERVATIONS

1 Time:
2 Time:
3 Time:
4 Time:
5 Time:
6 Time:
7 Time:
WEEKLY SUMMARY AND AVERAGES:

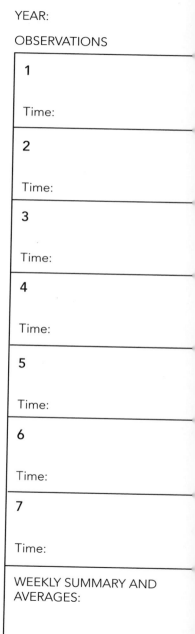

OBSERVATIONS

1 Time:				
2 Time:				
3 Time:				
4 Time:				
5 Time:				
6 Time:				
7 Time:				
WEEKLY SUMMARY AND AVERAGES:				

APRIL

YEAR:

OBSERVATIONS

8 Time:				
9 Time:				
10 Time:				
11 Time:				
12 Time:				
13 Time:				
14 Time:				
WEEKLY SUMMARY AND AVERAGES:				

YEAR:

OBSERVATIONS

8 Time:				
9 Time:				
10 Time:				
11 Time:				
12 Time:				
13 Time:				
14 Time:				
WEEKLY SUMMARY AND AVERAGES:				

OBSERVATIONS

8				
Time:				
9				
Time:				
10				
Time:				
11				
Time:				
12				
Time:				
13				
Time:				
14				
Time:				
WEEKLY SUMMARY AND AVERAGES:				

APRIL

OBSERVATIONS

YEAR:

OBSERVATIONS

15 Time:					15 Time:
16 Time:					16 Time:
17 Time:					17 Time:
18 Time:					18 Time:
19 Time:					19 Time:
20 Time:					20 Time:
21 Time:					21 Time:
WEEKLY SUMMARY AND AVERAGES:					WEEKLY SUMMARY AND AVERAGES:

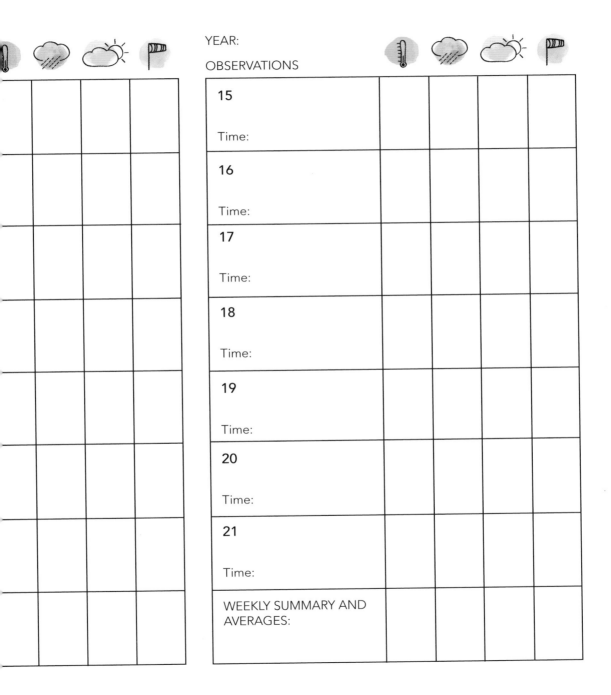

YEAR:

OBSERVATIONS

				15 Time:			
				16 Time:			
				17 Time:			
				18 Time:			
				19 Time:			
				20 Time:			
				21 Time:			
				WEEKLY SUMMARY AND AVERAGES:			

APRIL

OBSERVATIONS

22				
Time:				
23				
Time:				
24				
Time:				
25				
Time:				
26				
Time:				
27				
Time:				
28				
Time:				
WEEKLY SUMMARY AND AVERAGES:				

YEAR:

OBSERVATIONS

22				
Time:				
23				
Time:				
24				
Time:				
25				
Time:				
26				
Time:				
27				
Time:				
28				
Time:				
WEEKLY SUMMARY AND AVERAGES:				

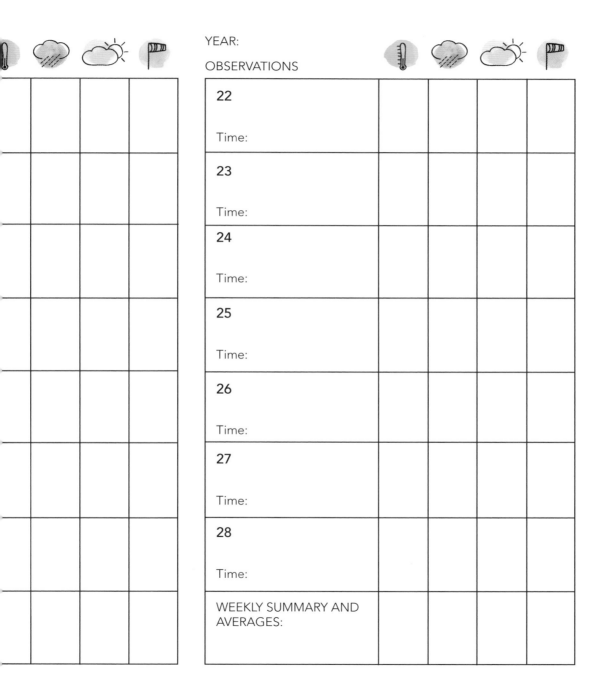

YEAR:

OBSERVATIONS

				22				
				Time:				
				23				
				Time:				
				24				
				Time:				
				25				
				Time:				
				26				
				Time:				
				27				
				Time:				
				28				
				Time:				
				WEEKLY SUMMARY AND AVERAGES:				

RAY OF LIGHT: SUN PILLARS

- Sun pillars are vertical beams of light projecting upwards or downwards from the sun when it is near the horizon.

- A sun pillar is the result of refraction and reflection of sunlight by ice crystals in the atmosphere.

- Around sunrise or sunset a sun pillar may be orange or red like the sunlight, but at other times it is white. Because the light forming the pillar is reflected, the pillar takes on that colour so that it is red or orange when close to the horizon and becomes yellow or white as the sun rises.

- Refraction of light through smaller prism-shaped ice-crystals can create other effects such as solar and lunar haloes, which are rings of light surrounding the sun or moon.

- The icy air of the Arctic and Antarctic often produces magnificent displays of sun pillars and haloes.

- There are many optical phenomena caused by water droplets, dust or ice. As well as sun pillars and rainbows, there are haloes, glares and coronas. Find out more about these from www.atoptics.co.uk

APRIL / MAY

YEAR:

OBSERVATIONS

29				
Time:				
30				
Time:				
1				
Time:				
2				
Time:				
3				
Time:				
4				
Time:				
5				
Time:				
WEEKLY SUMMARY AND AVERAGES:				

YEAR:

OBSERVATIONS

29
Time:
30
Time:
1
Time:
2
Time:
3
Time:
4
Time:
5
Time:
WEEKLY SUMMARY AND AVERAGES:

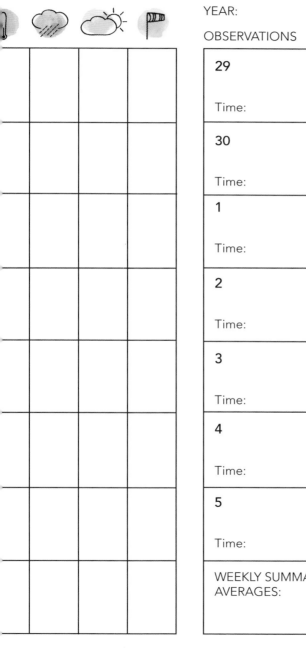

YEAR:

OBSERVATIONS

29 Time:				
30 Time:				
1 Time:				
2 Time:				
3 Time:				
4 Time:				
5 Time:				
WEEKLY SUMMARY AND AVERAGES:				

MAY

YEAR:

OBSERVATIONS

YEAR:

OBSERVATIONS

6 Time:					6 Time:				
7 Time:					7 Time:				
8 Time:					8 Time:				
9 Time:					9 Time:				
10 Time:					10 Time:				
11 Time:					11 Time:				
12 Time:					12 Time:				
WEEKLY SUMMARY AND AVERAGES:					WEEKLY SUMMARY AND AVERAGES:				

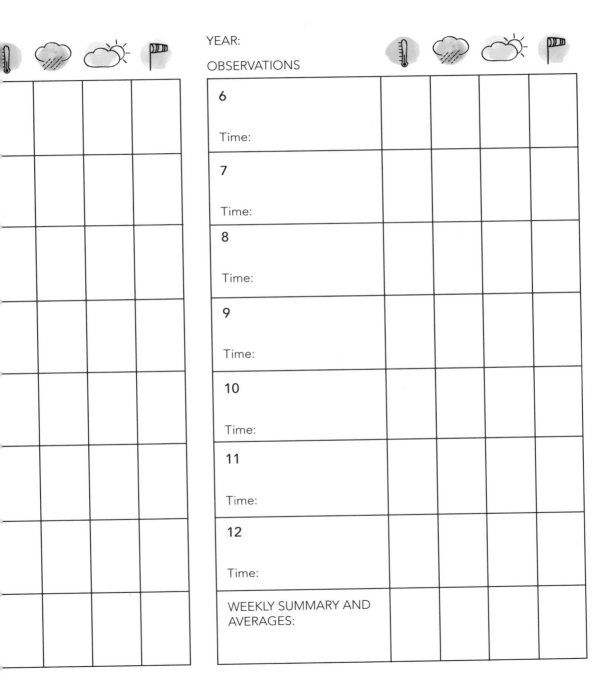

YEAR:

OBSERVATIONS

6 Time:				
7 Time:				
8 Time:				
9 Time:				
10 Time:				
11 Time:				
12 Time:				
WEEKLY SUMMARY AND AVERAGES:				

MAY

YEAR:

OBSERVATIONS

13 Time:				
14 Time:				
15 Time:				
16 Time:				
17 Time:				
18 Time:				
19 Time:				
WEEKLY SUMMARY AND AVERAGES:				

YEAR:

OBSERVATIONS

13 Time:				
14 Time:				
15 Time:				
16 Time:				
17 Time:				
18 Time:				
19 Time:				
WEEKLY SUMMARY AND AVERAGES:				

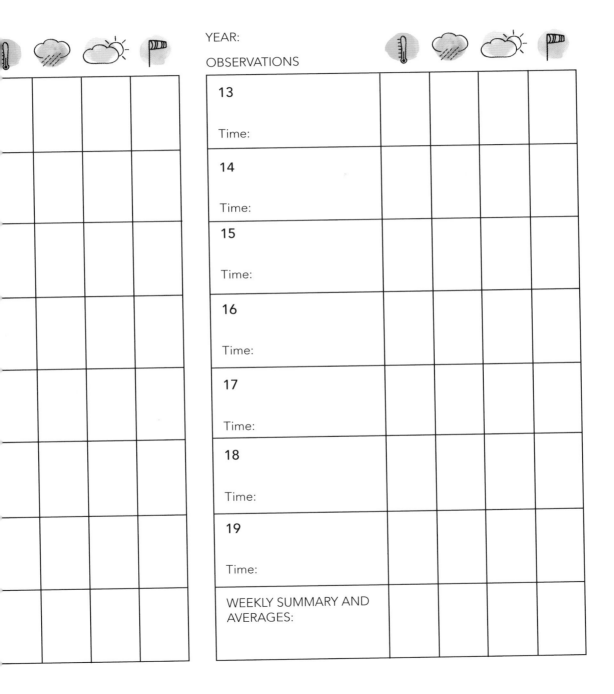

YEAR:

OBSERVATIONS

13 Time:				
14 Time:				
15 Time:				
16 Time:				
17 Time:				
18 Time:				
19 Time:				
WEEKLY SUMMARY AND AVERAGES:				

MAY

YEAR:

OBSERVATIONS

20 Time:				
21 Time:				
22 Time:				
23 Time:				
24 Time:				
25 Time:				
26 Time:				
WEEKLY SUMMARY AND AVERAGES:				

YEAR:

OBSERVATIONS

20 Time:
21 Time:
22 Time:
23 Time:
24 Time:
25 Time:
26 Time:
WEEKLY SUMMARY AND AVERAGES:

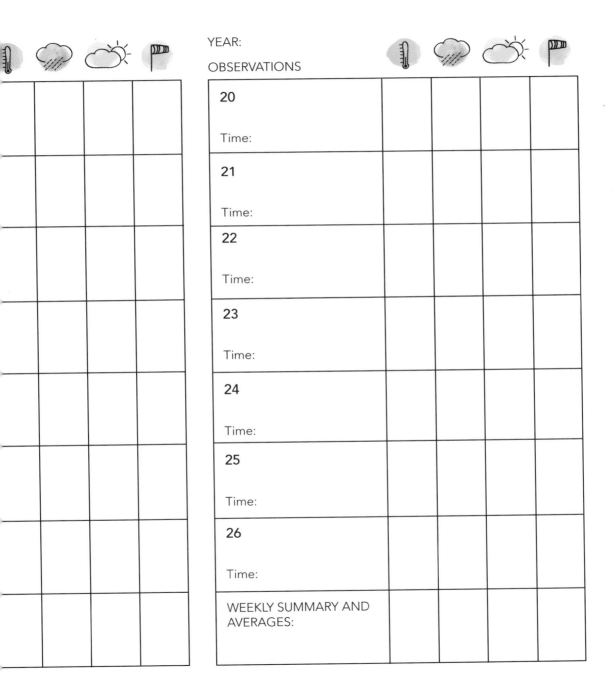

YEAR:

OBSERVATIONS

						20 Time:				
						21 Time:				
						22 Time:				
						23 Time:				
						24 Time:				
						25 Time:				
						26 Time:				
						WEEKLY SUMMARY AND AVERAGES:				

MAY / JUNE

YEAR:

OBSERVATIONS

27 Time:				
28 Time:				
29 Time:				
30 Time:				
31 Time:				
1 Time:				
2 Time:				
WEEKLY SUMMARY AND AVERAGES:				

YEAR:

OBSERVATIONS

27 Time:
28 Time:
29 Time:
30 Time:
31 Time:
1 Time:
2 Time:
WEEKLY SUMMARY AND AVERAGES:

YEAR:

OBSERVATIONS

27 Time:				
28 Time:				
29 Time:				
30 Time:				
31 Time:				
1 Time:				
2 Time:				
WEEKLY SUMMARY AND AVERAGES:				

RIBBONS IN THE SKY: CONTRAILS

o Contrails (an abbreviation of condensation trails) are lines of cloud made of water droplets or ice crystals that form in the wake of an aircraft. They are produced by condensation or freezing of the water vapour emitted from the aircraft's engines (water vapour is a product of fuel combustion).

o In air of low humidity, contrails disperse quickly but in moist air they persist for a long time, gradually thinning and spreading and becoming less distinct.

o The gap between the engines and the start of a contrail is a result of the air coming from the engines being too hot for condensation to occur immediately.

o Over the UK contrails only form at very high altitudes (usually above 8.5km (5.28 miles) in summer and 6km (3.73 miles) in winter) where the air temperature is below about -40°C (-40°F).

o Distrails (dissipation trails) are paths of clear air evaporated from a cloud by the heat of the engine exhaust as an aircraft passes through it.

o At high altitudes the vortices caused by the wing of an aircraft can produce a drop in temperature resulting in the formation of a contrail.

JUNE

YEAR:

OBSERVATIONS

3 Time:				
4 Time:				
5 Time:				
6 Time:				
7 Time:				
8 Time:				
9 Time:				
WEEKLY SUMMARY AND AVERAGES:				

YEAR:

OBSERVATIONS

3 Time:				
4 Time:				
5 Time:				
6 Time:				
7 Time:				
8 Time:				
9 Time:				
WEEKLY SUMMARY AND AVERAGES:				

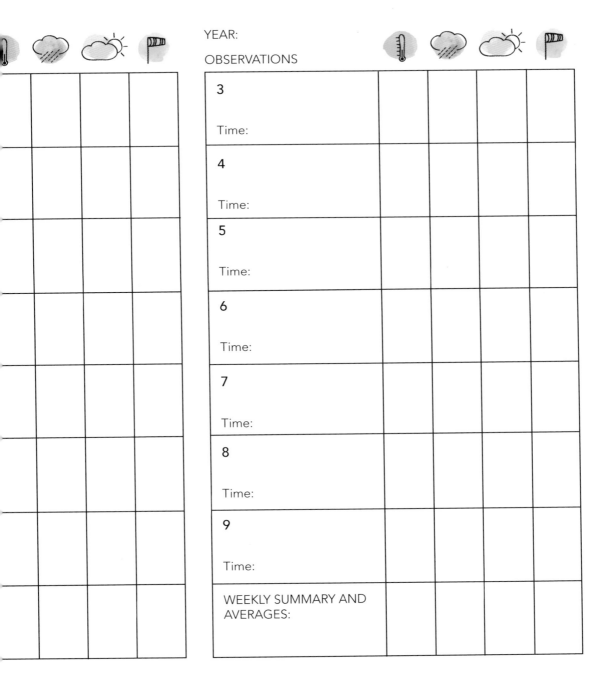

YEAR:

OBSERVATIONS

				3 Time:				
				4 Time:				
				5 Time:				
				6 Time:				
				7 Time:				
				8 Time:				
				9 Time:				
				WEEKLY SUMMARY AND AVERAGES:				

JUNE

YEAR:

OBSERVATIONS

10 Time:				
11 Time:				
12 Time:				
13 Time:				
14 Time:				
15 Time:				
16 Time:				
WEEKLY SUMMARY AND AVERAGES:				

YEAR:

OBSERVATIONS

10 Time:				
11 Time:				
12 Time:				
13 Time:				
14 Time:				
15 Time:				
16 Time:				
WEEKLY SUMMARY AND AVERAGES:				

YEAR:

OBSERVATIONS

10 Time:				
11 Time:				
12 Time:				
13 Time:				
14 Time:				
15 Time:				
16 Time:				
WEEKLY SUMMARY AND AVERAGES:				

JUNE

YEAR:

OBSERVATIONS

YEAR:

OBSERVATIONS

17				
Time:				
18				
Time:				
19				
Time:				
20				
Time:				
21				
Time:				
22				
Time:				
23				
Time:				
WEEKLY SUMMARY AND AVERAGES:				

17	
Time:	
18	
Time:	
19	
Time:	
20	
Time:	
21	
Time:	
22	
Time:	
23	
Time:	
WEEKLY SUMMARY AND AVERAGES:	

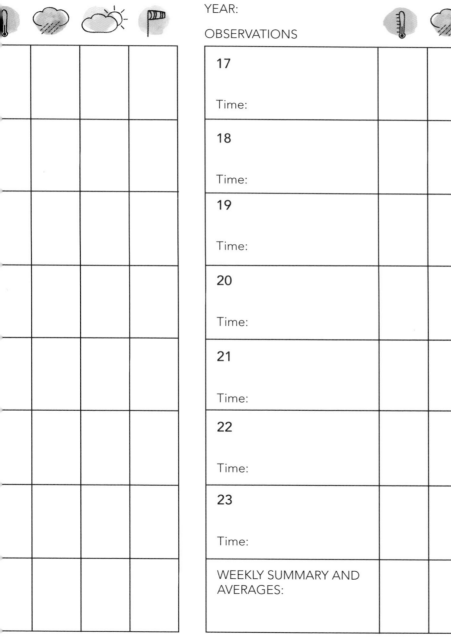

YEAR:

OBSERVATIONS

17 Time:				
18 Time:				
19 Time:				
20 Time:				
21 Time:				
22 Time:				
23 Time:				
WEEKLY SUMMARY AND AVERAGES:				

JUNE

YEAR:

OBSERVATIONS

24 Time:				
25 Time:				
26 Time:				
27 Time:				
28 Time:				
29 Time:				
30 Time:				
WEEKLY SUMMARY AND AVERAGES:				

YEAR:

OBSERVATIONS

24 Time:
25 Time:
26 Time:
27 Time:
28 Time:
29 Time:
30 Time:
WEEKLY SUMMARY AND AVERAGES:

				YEAR: OBSERVATIONS				
				24 Time:				
				25 Time:				
				26 Time:				
				27 Time:				
				28 Time:				
				29 Time:				
				30 Time:				
				WEEKLY SUMMARY AND AVERAGES:				

FORCE OF NATURE: HURRICANES

o The word 'hurricane' comes from Huracan, the Mayan god of wind, storm and fire. In the western Pacific Ocean the name 'typhoon' is used which comes from the Chinese for 'great wind'. Hurricanes and typhoons all belong to a class of weather systems called tropical cyclones.

o Hurricanes form over the tropical ocean and are usually between 200 and 1,000km (124 and 620 miles) in diameter. They consist of a mass of spiralling cloud.

o At the centre of a hurricane, there is a roughly circular area 20–65km (12–40 miles) in diameter where amounts of cloud are generally small and blue sky may sometimes be seen. This is known as the 'eye'.

o Hurricanes produce torrential rain and very strong winds – commonly more than 185km/h (115mph).

o A storm surge, which is caused by strong winds within the hurricane pushing water towards coasts and therefore raising sea-levels, is always a concern. These winds also create large waves which batter and weaken coastal structures.

o The tropical cyclone which affected the Ganges Delta of Bangladesh in 1970 is estimated to have caused over 300,000 deaths, with some estimates putting the figure as high as 1 million. The surge of water associated with the tropical cyclone was over 15 metres (50ft) and affected about 50 million people.

o Hurricane Katrina, which affected Louisiana and Mississippi in August 2005, is considered to be the worst natural disaster in the USA. The cost was estimated to be over $100 billion with at least 1,800 fatalities.

JULY

YEAR:

OBSERVATIONS

1 Time:				
2 Time:				
3 Time:				
4 Time:				
5 Time:				
6 Time:				
7 Time:				
WEEKLY SUMMARY AND AVERAGES:				

YEAR:

OBSERVATIONS

1 Time:
2 Time:
3 Time:
4 Time:
5 Time:
6 Time:
7 Time:
WEEKLY SUMMARY AND AVERAGES:

1 Time:				
2 Time:				
3 Time:				
4 Time:				
5 Time:				
6 Time:				
7 Time:				
WEEKLY SUMMARY AND AVERAGES:				

JULY

YEAR:

OBSERVATIONS

8 Time:				
9 Time:				
10 Time:				
11 Time:				
12 Time:				
13 Time:				
14 Time:				
WEEKLY SUMMARY AND AVERAGES:				

YEAR:

OBSERVATIONS

8 Time:
9 Time:
10 Time:
11 Time:
12 Time:
13 Time:
14 Time:
WEEKLY SUMMARY AND AVERAGES:

OBSERVATIONS

				8 Time:				
				9 Time:				
				10 Time:				
				11 Time:				
				12 Time:				
				13 Time:				
				14 Time:				
				WEEKLY SUMMARY AND AVERAGES:				

JULY

YEAR:

OBSERVATIONS

YEAR:

OBSERVATIONS

15 Time:					15 Time:				
16 Time:					16 Time:				
17 Time:					17 Time:				
18 Time:					18 Time:				
19 Time:					19 Time:				
20 Time:					20 Time:				
21 Time:					21 Time:				
WEEKLY SUMMARY AND AVERAGES:					WEEKLY SUMMARY AND AVERAGES:				

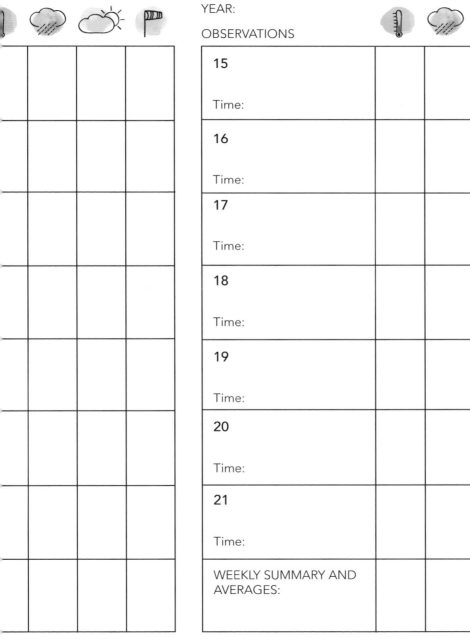

YEAR:

OBSERVATIONS

15 Time:				
16 Time:				
17 Time:				
18 Time:				
19 Time:				
20 Time:				
21 Time:				
WEEKLY SUMMARY AND AVERAGES:				

JULY

22 Time:				
23 Time:				
24 Time:				
25 Time:				
26 Time:				
27 Time:				
28 Time:				
WEEKLY SUMMARY AND AVERAGES:				

22 Time:
23 Time:
24 Time:
25 Time:
26 Time:
27 Time:
28 Time:
WEEKLY SUMMARY AND AVERAGES:

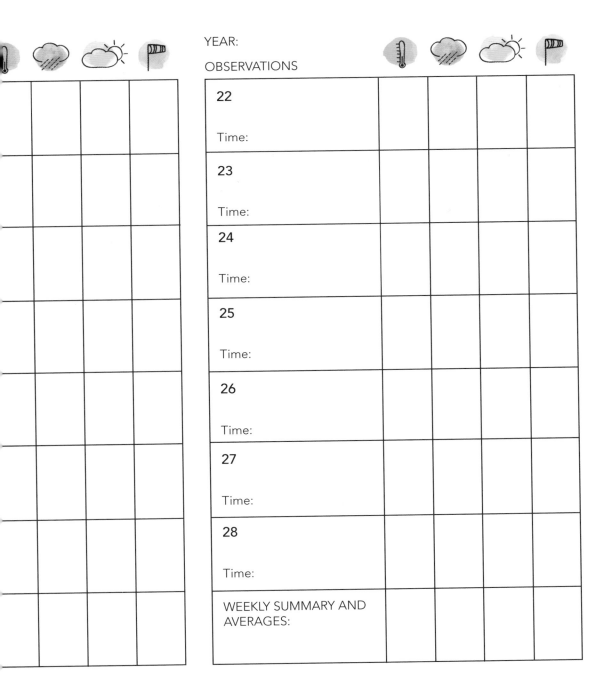

YEAR:

OBSERVATIONS

				22 Time:				
				23 Time:				
				24 Time:				
				25 Time:				
				26 Time:				
				27 Time:				
				28 Time:				
				WEEKLY SUMMARY AND AVERAGES:				

ALL IN A SPIN: TORNADOES

o A tornado is a violently rotating column of air extending from a cumulonimbus base to the ground.

o Windspeeds in a tornado may be as high as 483km/h (300mph).

o A tornado is often called a twister and this is not the same as a hurricane.

o Tornadoes are usually preceded by very heavy rain and sometimes hail. If hail falls from a thunderstorm, it is an indication that the storm has large amounts of energy and may be severe. In general, the larger the hailstones, the more potential for damaging thunderstorm winds and/or tornadoes.

o On 20 May 1949 a herd of 13 cows in Oklahoma was reportedly carried about 0.5km (0.31 miles) by a tornado before being dropped unharmed.

o On 21 November 1981 there were 105 tornadoes over the UK in just over five hours.

o A tornado in the middle of Birmingham, UK on 28 July 2005 injured 19 people, lifted cars and ripped out fences. However, city centres are not the natural habitat of a tornado; the tall buildings would normally stop their formation.

JULY / AUGUST

YEAR:

OBSERVATIONS

29 Time:				
30 Time:				
31 Time:				
1 Time:				
2 Time:				
3 Time:				
4 Time:				
WEEKLY SUMMARY AND AVERAGES:				

YEAR:

OBSERVATIONS

29 Time:
30 Time:
31 Time:
1 Time:
2 Time:
3 Time:
4 Time:
WEEKLY SUMMARY AND AVERAGES:

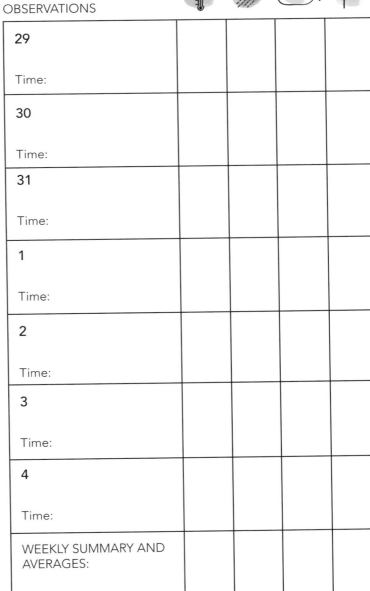

YEAR:

OBSERVATIONS

29				
Time:				
30				
Time:				
31				
Time:				
1				
Time:				
2				
Time:				
3				
Time:				
4				
Time:				
WEEKLY SUMMARY AND AVERAGES:				

AUGUST

YEAR:

OBSERVATIONS

5 Time:				
6 Time:				
7 Time:				
8 Time:				
9 Time:				
10 Time:				
11 Time:				
WEEKLY SUMMARY AND AVERAGES:				

YEAR:

OBSERVATIONS

5 Time:				
6 Time:				
7 Time:				
8 Time:				
9 Time:				
10 Time:				
11 Time:				
WEEKLY SUMMARY AND AVERAGES:				

OBSERVATIONS

					5				
					Time:				
					6				
					Time:				
					7				
					Time:				
					8				
					Time:				
					9				
					Time:				
					10				
					Time:				
					11				
					Time:				
					WEEKLY SUMMARY AND AVERAGES:				

AUGUST

YEAR:

OBSERVATIONS

12 Time:				
13 Time:				
14 Time:				
15 Time:				
16 Time:				
17 Time:				
18 Time:				
WEEKLY SUMMARY AND AVERAGES:				

YEAR:

OBSERVATIONS

12 Time:
13 Time:
14 Time:
15 Time:
16 Time:
17 Time:
18 Time:
WEEKLY SUMMARY AND AVERAGES:

YEAR:

OBSERVATIONS

12 Time:			
13 Time:			
14 Time:			
15 Time:			
16 Time:			
17 Time:			
18 Time:			
WEEKLY SUMMARY AND AVERAGES:			

AUGUST

YEAR:

OBSERVATIONS

19 Time:				
20 Time:				
21 Time:				
22 Time:				
23 Time:				
24 Time:				
25 Time:				
WEEKLY SUMMARY AND AVERAGES:				

YEAR:

OBSERVATIONS

19 Time:				
20 Time:				
21 Time:				
22 Time:				
23 Time:				
24 Time:				
25 Time:				
WEEKLY SUMMARY AND AVERAGES:				

YEAR:

OBSERVATIONS

19 Time:				
20 Time:				
21 Time:				
22 Time:				
23 Time:				
24 Time:				
25 Time:				
WEEKLY SUMMARY AND AVERAGES:				

AUGUST / SEPTEMBER

YEAR:

OBSERVATIONS

26 Time:				
27 Time:				
28 Time:				
29 Time:				
30 Time:				
31 Time:				
1 Time:				
WEEKLY SUMMARY AND AVERAGES:				

YEAR:

OBSERVATIONS

26 Time:
27 Time:
28 Time:
29 Time:
30 Time:
31 Time:
1 Time:
WEEKLY SUMMARY AND AVERAGES:

YEAR:

OBSERVATIONS

26 Time:				
27 Time:				
28 Time:				
29 Time:				
30 Time:				
31 Time:				
1 Time:				
WEEKLY SUMMARY AND AVERAGES:				

GIANT OF THE SKIES: CUMULONIMBUS

o   A mature cumulonimbus cloud is a near-vertical column, which
    spreads out at the top to resemble a blacksmith's anvil. The anvil
    can stretch out for hundreds of kilometres and consists of ice
    crystals rather than water droplets.

o   These clouds can be as high as 10,000m (33,000ft) in the UK, more
    than seven times the height of Ben Nevis.

o   They produce heavy showers, sometimes accompanied by thunder
    and lightning, hail and strong gusts of wind.

o   A cumulonimbus develops out of a cumulus cloud. Typically it lasts
    approximately one hour and is about 5km (3.1 miles) in diameter.

o   A 'supercell' is a rare but particularly violent long-lived
    thunderstorm. Supercells commonly produce large hail and high
    winds, and sometimes spawn tornadoes.

o   The heaviest rainfall in the UK comes from thunderstorms. In
    extreme cases more than 152mm (6in) of rain can fall in three hours.

o   During the spring and summer, cumulonimbus clouds tend to form
    in the afternoon and evening due to the heating of the Earth's
    surface. These clouds may also occur along the boundary of a
    cold front.

SEPTEMBER

YEAR:

OBSERVATIONS

2 Time:				
3 Time:				
4 Time:				
5 Time:				
6 Time:				
7 Time:				
8 Time:				
WEEKLY SUMMARY AND AVERAGES:				

YEAR:

OBSERVATIONS

2 Time:
3 Time:
4 Time:
5 Time:
6 Time:
7 Time:
8 Time:
WEEKLY SUMMARY AND AVERAGES:

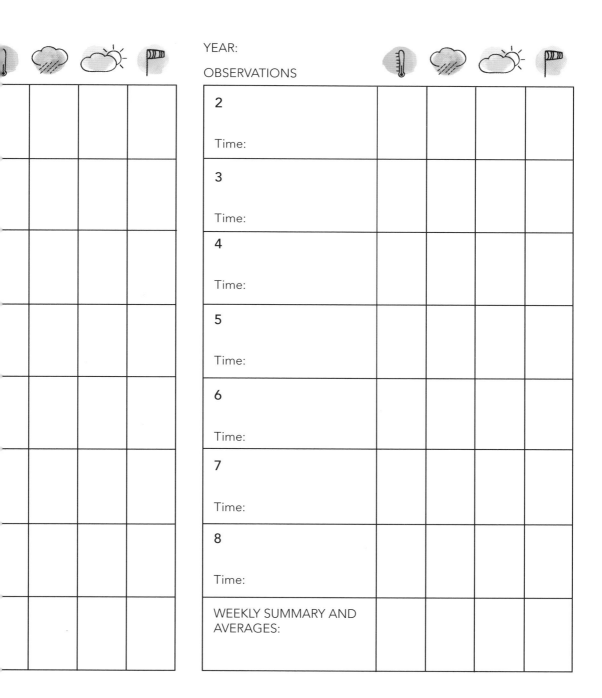

YEAR:

OBSERVATIONS

2 Time:				
3 Time:				
4 Time:				
5 Time:				
6 Time:				
7 Time:				
8 Time:				
WEEKLY SUMMARY AND AVERAGES:				

SEPTEMBER

YEAR:

OBSERVATIONS

9				
Time:				
10				
Time:				
11				
Time:				
12				
Time:				
13				
Time:				
14				
Time:				
15				
Time:				
WEEKLY SUMMARY AND AVERAGES:				

YEAR:

OBSERVATIONS

9
Time:
10
Time:
11
Time:
12
Time:
13
Time:
14
Time:
15
Time:
WEEKLY SUMMARY AND AVERAGES:

				YEAR:				
				OBSERVATIONS				
				9 Time:				
				10 Time:				
				11 Time:				
				12 Time:				
				13 Time:				
				14 Time:				
				15 Time:				
				WEEKLY SUMMARY AND AVERAGES:				

SEPTEMBER

YEAR:

OBSERVATIONS

16 Time:				
17 Time:				
18 Time:				
19 Time:				
20 Time:				
21 Time:				
22 Time:				
WEEKLY SUMMARY AND AVERAGES:				

YEAR:

OBSERVATIONS

16 Time:
17 Time:
18 Time:
19 Time:
20 Time:
21 Time:
22 Time:
WEEKLY SUMMARY AND AVERAGES:

YEAR:

OBSERVATIONS

16 Time:				
17 Time:				
18 Time:				
19 Time:				
20 Time:				
21 Time:				
22 Time:				
WEEKLY SUMMARY AND AVERAGES:				

SEPTEMBER

YEAR:

OBSERVATIONS

23 Time:				
24 Time:				
25 Time:				
26 Time:				
27 Time:				
28 Time:				
29 Time:				
WEEKLY SUMMARY AND AVERAGES:				

YEAR:

OBSERVATIONS

23 Time:				
24 Time:				
25 Time:				
26 Time:				
27 Time:				
28 Time:				
29 Time:				
WEEKLY SUMMARY AND AVERAGES:				

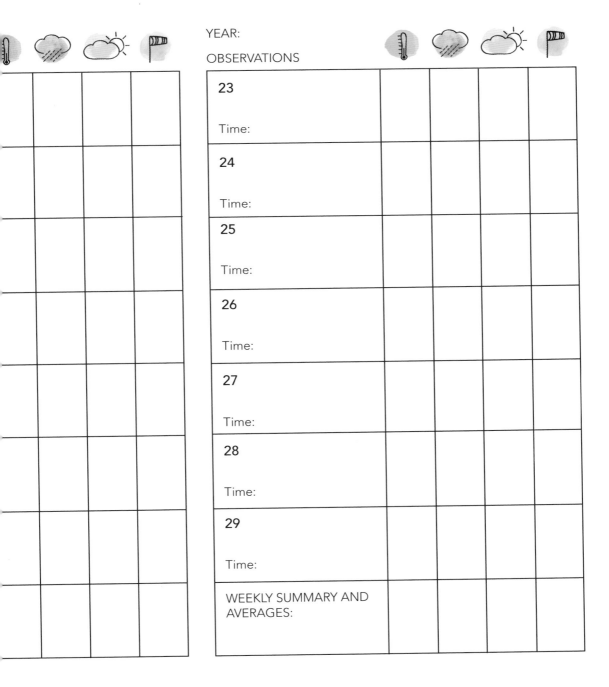

YEAR:

OBSERVATIONS

23 Time:				
24 Time:				
25 Time:				
26 Time:				
27 Time:				
28 Time:				
29 Time:				
WEEKLY SUMMARY AND AVERAGES:				

A LOW CLOUD: FOG

o   Fog is a visible suspension of water droplets near the ground which obscures surface visibility. By international agreement visibility of less that 1km (0.62 miles) is referred to as fog for aviation purposes. Reference to fog in general weather forecasts indicates a visibility of less than 200m (650ft).

o   The only physical difference between fog and cloud is that cloud has its base above the ground. In other words fog is cloud at ground level.

o   The term mist is used when the visibility is reduced by suspended water droplets but it is still 1km (0.62 miles) or more.

o   The term haze is used, whatever the horizontal visibility, when the visibility is reduced by very small, dry, solid particles suspended in the atmosphere.

o   Fog forms when the air near the ground is cooled from below to such an extent that condensation takes place.

o   The two main types of fog are advection fog and radiation fog. Advection fog forms when moist air is carried by the wind over a cold surface such as the sea or frozen ground. Radiation fog is most common in the autumn and after dark as the ground cools. It occurs when there is a clear sky with the air being still with sufficient moisture.

o   In the UK radiation fog is most likely to form in inland areas during November, December and January. However, advection fog tends to occur in early spring in mild south-westerly winds.

SEPTEMBER / OCTOBER

YEAR:

OBSERVATIONS

30 Time:				
1 Time:				
2 Time:				
3 Time:				
4 Time:				
5 Time:				
6 Time:				
WEEKLY SUMMARY AND AVERAGES:				

YEAR:

OBSERVATIONS

30 Time:
1 Time:
2 Time:
3 Time:
4 Time:
5 Time:
6 Time:
WEEKLY SUMMARY AND AVERAGES:

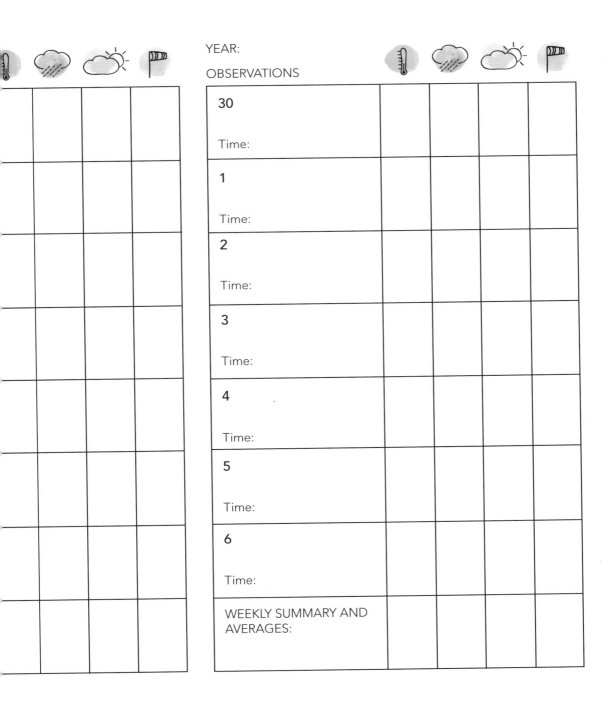

YEAR:

OBSERVATIONS

					30 Time:				
					1 Time:				
					2 Time:				
					3 Time:				
					4 Time:				
					5 Time:				
					6 Time:				
					WEEKLY SUMMARY AND AVERAGES:				

OCTOBER

YEAR:

OBSERVATIONS

7 Time:				
8 Time:				
9 Time:				
10 Time:				
11 Time:				
12 Time:				
13 Time:				
WEEKLY SUMMARY AND AVERAGES:				

YEAR:

OBSERVATIONS

7 Time:
8 Time:
9 Time:
10 Time:
11 Time:
12 Time:
13 Time:
WEEKLY SUMMARY AND AVERAGES:

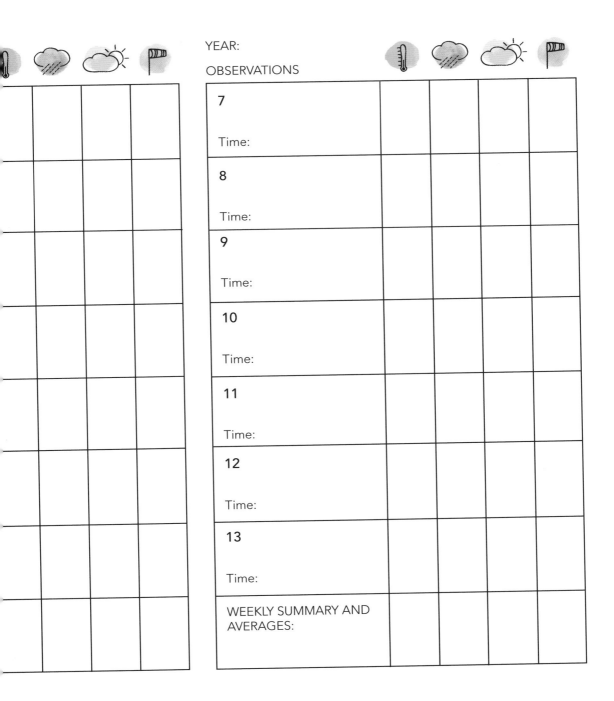

YEAR:

OBSERVATIONS

7 Time:				
8 Time:				
9 Time:				
10 Time:				
11 Time:				
12 Time:				
13 Time:				
WEEKLY SUMMARY AND AVERAGES:				

OCTOBER

14 Time:					14 Time:			
15 Time:					15 Time:			
16 Time:					16 Time:			
17 Time:					17 Time:			
18 Time:					18 Time:			
19 Time:					19 Time:			
20 Time:					20 Time:			
WEEKLY SUMMARY AND AVERAGES:					WEEKLY SUMMARY AND AVERAGES:			

YEAR:

OBSERVATIONS

14 Time:				
15 Time:				
16 Time:				
17 Time:				
18 Time:				
19 Time:				
20 Time:				
WEEKLY SUMMARY AND AVERAGES:				

OCTOBER

YEAR:

OBSERVATIONS

21 Time:				
22 Time:				
23 Time:				
24 Time:				
25 Time:				
26 Time:				
27 Time:				
WEEKLY SUMMARY AND AVERAGES:				

YEAR:

OBSERVATIONS

21 Time:
22 Time:
23 Time:
24 Time:
25 Time:
26 Time:
27 Time:
WEEKLY SUMMARY AND AVERAGES:

OBSERVATIONS

21				
Time:				
22				
Time:				
23				
Time:				
24				
Time:				
25				
Time:				
26				
Time:				
27				
Time:				
WEEKLY SUMMARY AND AVERAGES:				

OCTOBER / NOVEMBER

YEAR:

OBSERVATIONS

28 Time:				
29 Time:				
30 Time:				
31 Time:				
1 Time:				
2 Time:				
3 Time:				
WEEKLY SUMMARY AND AVERAGES:				

YEAR:

OBSERVATIONS

28 Time:
29 Time:
30 Time:
31 Time:
1 Time:
2 Time:
3 Time:
WEEKLY SUMMARY AND AVERAGES:

OBSERVATIONS

28 Time:				
29 Time:				
30 Time:				
31 Time:				
1 Time:				
2 Time:				
3 Time:				
WEEKLY SUMMARY AND AVERAGES:				

MOVEMENTS OF THE AIR: WIND

- Winds are horizontal movements of air. The speed and direction of the wind are mainly determined by differences in pressure and the Earth's rotation.

- Variations in pressure are shown on maps by isobars. These are lines joining places of equal pressure. The closer together the isobars the stronger the wind. The winds blow almost parallel to the isobars.

- Winds are described in terms of their speed and the direction from which they are blowing. A westerly wind for example blows from the west towards the east.

- In the northern hemisphere winds blow clockwise around a high pressure area and anticlockwise around a low pressure area.

- It has been estimated that the storm which affected southern England on 16 October 1987 uprooted 15 million trees.

- The windiest place in the world is eastern Adélie Land on the coast of Antarctica. Strong winds blow for approximately 300 days per year down off the icecap towards the sea, reaching more than 120km/h (75mph) on one day out of three.

- The highest gust recorded at a low-level site in the UK was 228km/h (142mph) at Fraserburgh, Aberdeenshire, on 13 February 1989. At a high-level site over 270km/h (167mph) has been recorded.

NOVEMBER

OBSERVATIONS

OBSERVATIONS

4 Time:					4 Time:
5 Time:					5 Time:
6 Time:					6 Time:
7 Time:					7 Time:
8 Time:					8 Time:
9 Time:					9 Time:
10 Time:					10 Time:
WEEKLY SUMMARY AND AVERAGES:					WEEKLY SUMMARY AND AVERAGES:

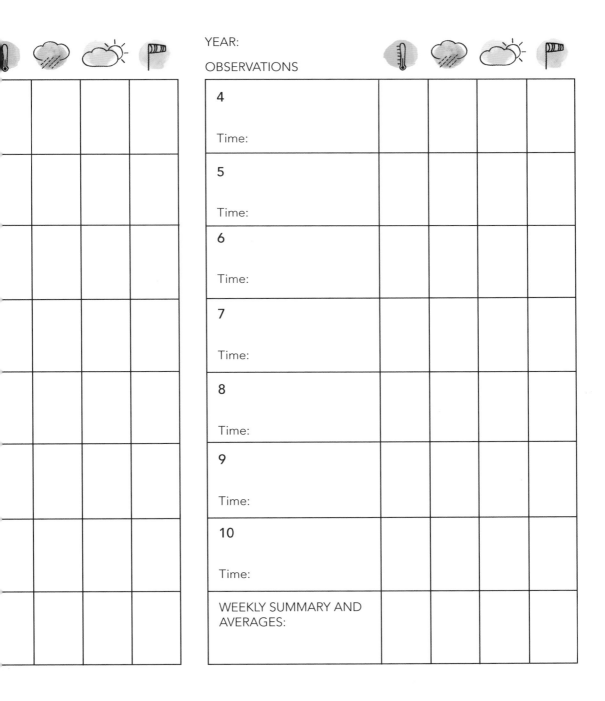

YEAR:

OBSERVATIONS

				4 Time:			
				5 Time:			
				6 Time:			
				7 Time:			
				8 Time:			
				9 Time:			
				10 Time:			
				WEEKLY SUMMARY AND AVERAGES:			

NOVEMBER

YEAR:

OBSERVATIONS

11 Time:				
12 Time:				
13 Time:				
14 Time:				
15 Time:				
16 Time:				
17 Time:				
WEEKLY SUMMARY AND AVERAGES:				

YEAR:

OBSERVATIONS

11 Time:
12 Time:
13 Time:
14 Time:
15 Time:
16 Time:
17 Time:
WEEKLY SUMMARY AND AVERAGES:

YEAR:

OBSERVATIONS

				11 Time:			
				12 Time:			
				13 Time:			
				14 Time:			
				15 Time:			
				16 Time:			
				17 Time:			
				WEEKLY SUMMARY AND AVERAGES:			

NOVEMBER

OBSERVATIONS

18 Time:				
19 Time:				
20 Time:				
21 Time:				
22 Time:				
23 Time:				
24 Time:				
WEEKLY SUMMARY AND AVERAGES:				

YEAR:

OBSERVATIONS

18 Time:				
19 Time:				
20 Time:				
21 Time:				
22 Time:				
23 Time:				
24 Time:				
WEEKLY SUMMARY AND AVERAGES:				

18 Time:				
19 Time:				
20 Time:				
21 Time:				
22 Time:				
23 Time:				
24 Time:				
WEEKLY SUMMARY AND AVERAGES:				

NOVEMBER / DECEMBER

YEAR:

OBSERVATIONS

25 Time:				
26 Time:				
27 Time:				
28 Time:				
29 Time:				
30 Time:				
1 Time:				
WEEKLY SUMMARY AND AVERAGES:				

YEAR:

OBSERVATIONS

25   Time:
26   Time:
27   Time:
28   Time:
29   Time:
30   Time:
1   Time:
WEEKLY SUMMARY AND AVERAGES:

OBSERVATIONS

					25 Time:				
					26 Time:				
					27 Time:				
					28 Time:				
					29 Time:				
					30 Time:				
					1 Time:				
					WEEKLY SUMMARY AND AVERAGES:				

SNOW BUSINESS: SNOW

o Snow starts high in the frozen tops of large thick clouds
   as minute ice crystals that form in very low temperatures
   (below -40°C (-40°F)). These crystals grow into beautifully
   symmetrical 'snowflakes'.

o Ice crystals and snowflakes come in a variety of forms – needles,
   hexagons, columns, prisms and six-pointed stars depending on
   the temperature of the air through which they fall. They all have
   a six-sided geometry, however.

o 30cm (12in) of fresh snow is about the same water equivalence
   as 25mm (1in) of rainfall.

o On low ground in the UK falling snow is normally limited to
   the period October to April, with snow seldom lying before
   December or after March.

o A flurry is a period of light snow with little accumulation. On the
   other hand, a blizzard is a long-lasting snow storm with intense
   snowfall and high wind.

o 12% of the Earth's land surface is permanently covered by ice
   and snow.

DECEMBER

OBSERVATIONS

2 Time:				
3 Time:				
4 Time:				
5 Time:				
6 Time:				
7 Time:				
8 Time:				
WEEKLY SUMMARY AND AVERAGES:				

YEAR:

OBSERVATIONS

2 Time:				
3 Time:				
4 Time:				
5 Time:				
6 Time:				
7 Time:				
8 Time:				
WEEKLY SUMMARY AND AVERAGES:				

2 Time:				
3 Time:				
4 Time:				
5 Time:				
6 Time:				
7 Time:				
8 Time:				
WEEKLY SUMMARY AND AVERAGES:				

DECEMBER

OBSERVATIONS

9 Time:				
10 Time:				
11 Time:				
12 Time:				
13 Time:				
14 Time:				
15 Time:				
WEEKLY SUMMARY AND AVERAGES:				

YEAR:

OBSERVATIONS

9 Time:				
10 Time:				
11 Time:				
12 Time:				
13 Time:				
14 Time:				
15 Time:				
WEEKLY SUMMARY AND AVERAGES:				

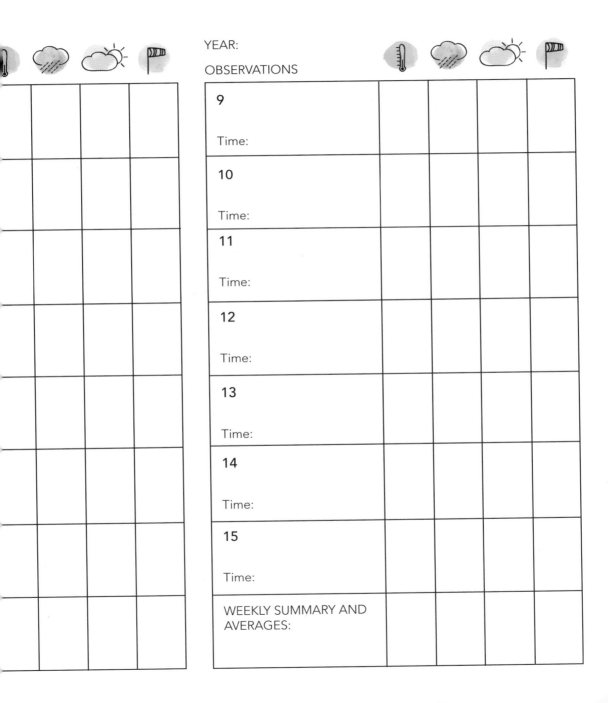

YEAR:

OBSERVATIONS

				9 Time:				
				10 Time:				
				11 Time:				
				12 Time:				
				13 Time:				
				14 Time:				
				15 Time:				
				WEEKLY SUMMARY AND AVERAGES:				

DECEMBER

YEAR:

OBSERVATIONS

16 Time:				
17 Time:				
18 Time:				
19 Time:				
20 Time:				
21 Time:				
22 Time:				
WEEKLY SUMMARY AND AVERAGES:				

YEAR:

OBSERVATIONS

16 Time:
17 Time:
18 Time:
19 Time:
20 Time:
21 Time:
22 Time:
WEEKLY SUMMARY AND AVERAGES:

OBSERVATIONS

16 Time:				
17 Time:				
18 Time:				
19 Time:				
20 Time:				
21 Time:				
22 Time:				
WEEKLY SUMMARY AND AVERAGES:				

DECEMBER

YEAR:

OBSERVATIONS

YEAR:

OBSERVATIONS

23					23				
Time:					Time:				
24					24				
Time:					Time:				
25					25				
Time:					Time:				
26					26				
Time:					Time:				
27					27				
Time:					Time:				
28					28				
Time:					Time:				
29					29				
Time:					Time:				
WEEKLY SUMMARY AND AVERAGES:					WEEKLY SUMMARY AND AVERAGES:				

OBSERVATIONS

23 Time:				
24 Time:				
25 Time:				
26 Time:				
27 Time:				
28 Time:				
29 Time:				
WEEKLY SUMMARY AND AVERAGES:				

DECEMBER

YEAR:

OBSERVATIONS

30 Time:				
31 Time:				

YEAR:

OBSERVATIONS

30 Time:				
31 Time:				

YEAR:

OBSERVATIONS

30 Time:				
31 Time:				

ANNUAL SUMMARIES

It can be interesting to calculate the average of any of the weekly records you have been keeping and transfer them to the annual summaries in the following pages. You will then get a much better sense of the bigger picture and how weather patterns and the climate may be changing.

Don't worry if you have missed recording some days, as you can just use the average of the days you have recorded in that week and make a note in the Comments column to remind yourself about what data you have used.

Sometimes we want to record observations that don't fall neatly into a particular type of record. Use the notes section in the following pages to record any observations of this type or thoughts about what you have been doing.

Use the graph paper if you want to plot changes in a particular area.

YEAR 1

YEAR:  COMMENTS:

JANUARY					
FEBRUARY					
MARCH					
APRIL					
MAY					
JUNE					
JULY					
AUGUST					
SEPTEMBER					
OCTOBER					
NOVEMBER					
DECEMBER					

YEAR 1: GENERAL OBSERVATIONS AND CONCLUSIONS

NOTES

YEAR 2

YEAR:  COMMENTS:

JANUARY					
FEBRUARY					
MARCH					
APRIL					
MAY					
JUNE					
JULY					
AUGUST					
SEPTEMBER					
OCTOBER					
NOVEMBER					
DECEMBER					

YEAR 2: GENERAL OBSERVATIONS AND CONCLUSIONS

NOTES

YEAR 3

YEAR:    COMMENTS:

JANUARY					
FEBRUARY					
MARCH					
APRIL					
MAY					
JUNE					
JULY					
AUGUST					
SEPTEMBER					
OCTOBER					
NOVEMBER					
DECEMBER					

YEAR 3: GENERAL OBSERVATIONS AND CONCLUSIONS

NOTES

GRAPHS

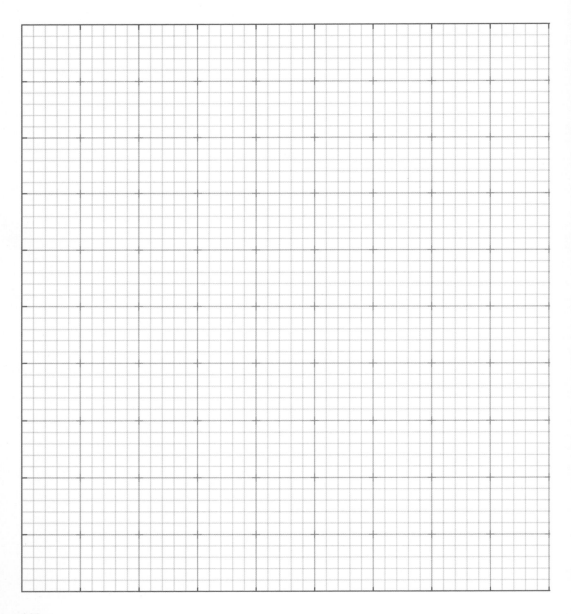

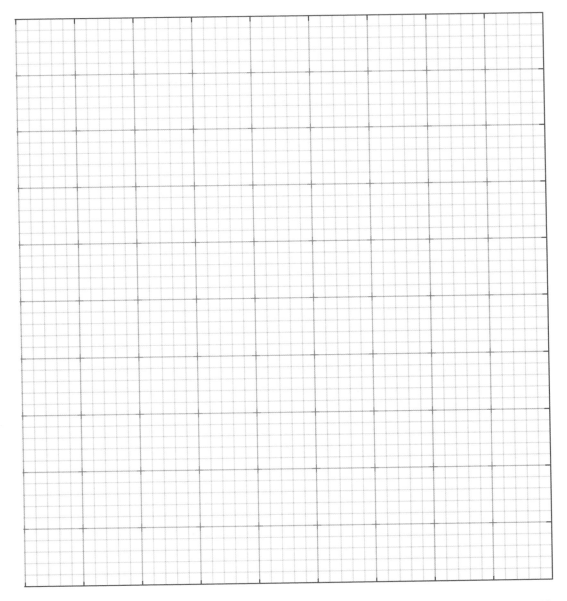

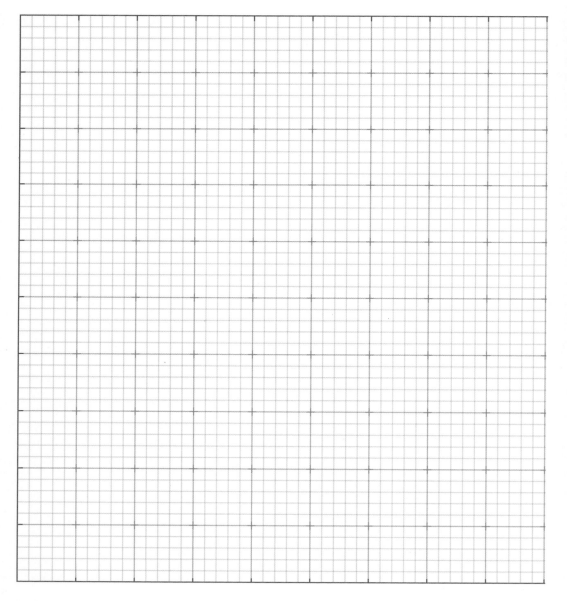

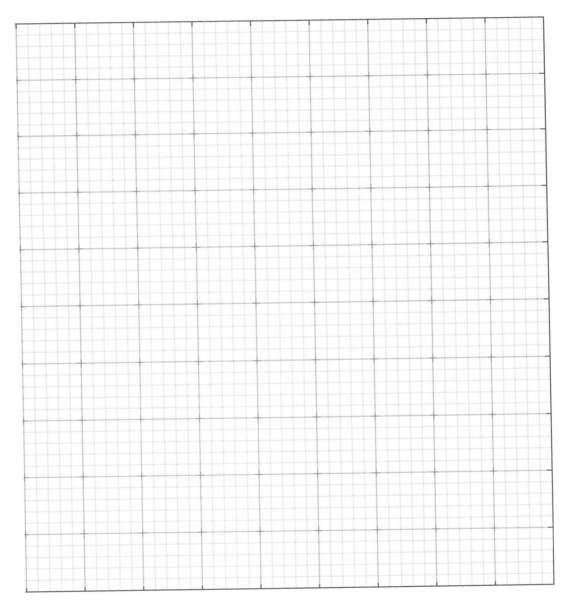

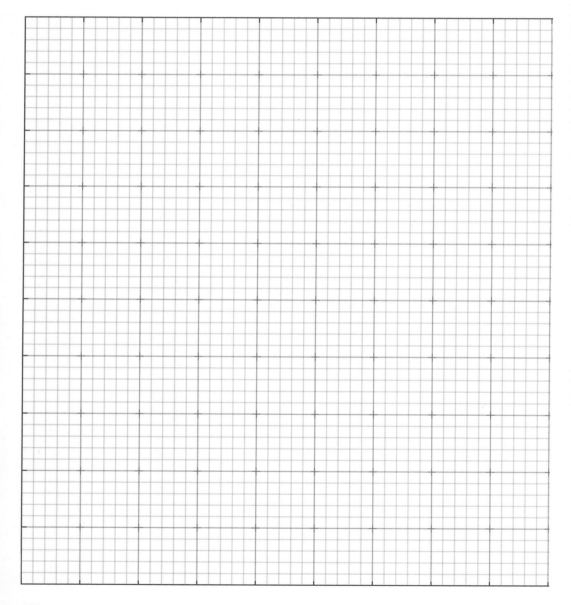

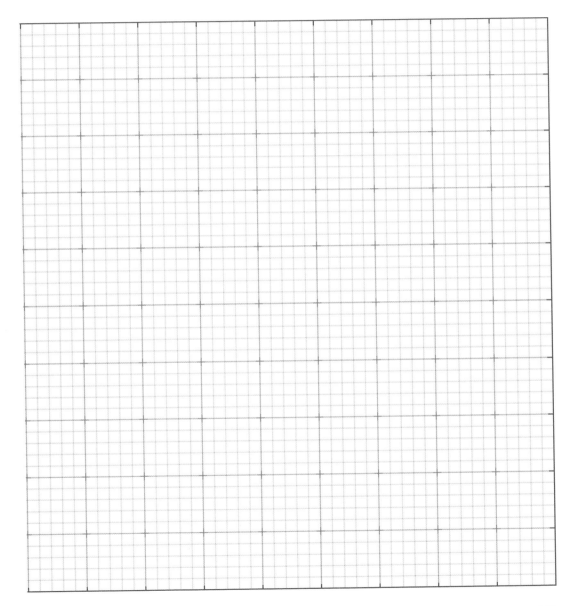

GLOSSARY

Acid rain: Rain that is more acidic than normal because water vapour has condensed on to particles of sulphate or nitrogen oxide.

Advection: The transfer of some property (e.g. temperature or moisture) by the horizontal movement of air or water, such as a wind or ocean current.

Advection fog: Fog caused by the condensation of water vapour when warm, moist air crosses cold ground or sea.

Air: A naturally occurring mixture of gases, chiefly nitrogen and oxygen with small amounts of argon, carbon dioxide, and water vapour – we sometimes call this our atmosphere.

Air pressure: The weight of the atmosphere pressing down on the Earth's surface as a result of gravity.

Anemometer: An instrument for measuring the speed of wind.

Anticyclone: A large area of high atmospheric pressure, characterized by outward-spiralling winds – a 'high'. In the northern hemisphere, winds rotate around an anticyclone in a clockwise direction.

Barometer: An instrument for measuring atmospheric pressure.

Beaufort scale: A scale that indicates wind speed by the effect wind has on familiar objects.

Black ice: Transparent ice that forms when liquid water freezes on the ground.

Celsius: A scale of temperature based on one introduced in 1742 by Celsius, a Swedish astronomer and physicist, who divided the interval between the freezing and boiling points of water into 100 parts. The present system, where the freezing point is marked 0 and the boiling point is marked 100, was introduced by Christin of Lyons in 1743.

Climate: The long-term (often taken as 30 years) average weather pattern of a region.

Cloud: A structure formed in the atmosphere by condensed water vapour.

Cold front: The boundary between two different air masses where the cold air pushes the warm air out of the way and brings colder weather.

Condensation: The process by which water vapour becomes liquid water.

Conduction: The process of heat transfer through materials by molecular motion.

Convection: The process of heat transfer through fluids by means of rising currents.

Coriolis force: An effect caused by the Earth's rotation, which causes winds and currents to follow a curved path across the Earth's surface – to the right (clockwise) in the northern hemisphere, to the left (anticlockwise) in the southern hemisphere.

Cyclone: A large area of low atmospheric pressure, characterized by inward-spiralling winds often called a 'low' or a 'depression'. Also the name used for a hurricane in the Indian Ocean and Western Pacific.

Depression: A low-pressure weather system.

Dew: Liquid water that has condensed on to objects at or near the Earth's surface.

Dew point: The temperature at which water starts to condense out of a particular air mass.

Downburst: A strong downdraught of short duration produced by some thunderstorms.

Evaporation: The process where liquid water turns into vapour (e.g. a rain puddle may evaporate into water vapour when

the sun comes out). It is the opposite of 'condensation'.

Fahrenheit: A scale of temperature introduced in about 1709 by the German physicist, Fahrenheit, who was the first to use mercury as the thermometric substance. Primary fixed points were the temperatures of a mixture of common salt and ice and the temperature of the human body; with reference to these the freezing point of water was marked 32 degrees, and the boiling point of water was marked 212 degrees.

Fog: Water droplets in the air that reduce visibility to less than 1,000m (1,100 yards).

Front: The boundary between two air masses.

Frost: White ice crystals deposited on the surface of objects that have a temperature below the freezing point of water.

Hail: Pieces of hard, solid ice falling from clouds.

Hemisphere: One half of a sphere. The term is usually applied to regions north or south of the equator.

High: Also known as an 'anticyclone' – an area of high air pressure with a system of winds rotating outwards. This usually means dry weather.

Humidity: The amount of water vapour in the air.

Hurricane: A tropical revolving storm with sustained wind speeds of more than 118km/h (73mph). It is called a hurricane in the North Atlantic, but in other parts of the world it is known as a typhoon or tropical cyclone.

Isobar: A line on a map or chart that links points of equal atmospheric pressure.

Jet stream: A strong, high-level wind that can reach speeds in excess of 320km/h (200mph) – it is usually around 5–10km (3–6 miles) above the ground.

Katabatic wind: A wind which blows down a slope.

Latitude: Position on the Earth's surface north or south of the equator.

Lee: The side of a mountain, hillside, or island that is facing away from the prevailing wind.

Lightning: Discharge of static electricity in the atmosphere, usually between the ground and a storm cloud.

Longitude: Position on the Earth's surface east or west of the Greenwich meridian.

Low: Also called a 'depression' – this region of low pressure can mean wet weather – it is the opposite of 'high' pressure or 'anticyclone'.

Meteorologist: Someone who makes a scientific study of weather, weather processes and/or the climate.

Meteorology: The science of the atmosphere – meteorology embraces both weather and climate and is concerned with all aspects of the Earth's atmosphere (and those of the planets) and with the interaction between the atmosphere and the surface. The term was first used by Aristotle.

Millibar: International unit for measuring air pressure. Now a hectopascal (hPa) is the standard unit for pressure.

Monsoon: The seasonal shift in wind direction that brings alternate very wet and very dry seasons to India and much of South-east Asia.

Occluded front: The combination of warm and cold fronts as a cold front overtakes a warm front. The front develops during the later stages of the life cycle of a frontal depression and is so called because of the associated occluding (shutting off) the warm air from the Earth's surface.

Precipitation: Moisture that is released from the atmosphere as rain, drizzle, hail, sleet or snow.

Radiation: Process by which energy travels across space.

Sea-level: The normal level of high-tide, used as a baseline for measuring height or depth.

Snowline: The vertical limit of snow lying on mountain sides throughout the year.

Synoptic chart: A map showing large-scale weather patterns in an area at a given time.

Typhoon: A name of Chinese origin (meaning 'great wind') applied to the intense tropical cyclones which occur in the western Pacific Ocean. They are the same as the hurricanes of the Atlantic Ocean and the cyclones of the Bay of Bengal.

Warm front: The boundary between two different air masses where warm air pushes cold air away to bring warmer weather.

Water vapour: Water in its gas form. One of the most important constituents of the atmosphere. Caused by evaporation at the Earth's surface the concentration of water vapour tends to decrease fairly steadily with height. Warm air is able to hold more water vapour, whilst cold air has less water vapour.

Royal Meteorological Society (www.rmets.org)
This site provides information about the Society's work, including its publications, meetings, specialist groups and educational activities.

Met Office (www.metoffice.gov.uk)
This is the UK's national meteorological service, which provides weather forecasts, shipping bulletins, educational material and information about climate change. WOW (Weather Observations Website www.wowmetoffice.gov.uk) is an online platform to share weather observations.

BBC Weather Centre (www.bbc.co.uk/weather)
This site provides a one-stop shop for weather information including world weather, UK weather forecasts, charts and weather images. BBC Weather Watchers (www.bbc.co.uk/weatherwatchers) is an online platform to share weather observations.

Tornado and Storm Research Organisation (www.torro.org.uk)
TORRO is a tornado and storm research body with activities in data collection, site investigations and climatological research.

Cloud Appreciation Society (www.cloudappreciationsociety.org)
A website dedicated to appreciating clouds through pictures, poetry and publications.

European Centre for Medium Range Weather Forecasts (www.ecmwf.int)

This site provides information about the work of ECMWF and access to charts showing surface and upper-air forecasts for three to six days ahead.

EUMETSAT (www.eumetsat.int)

This site provides information about the activities of the European Organization for the Exploitation of Meteorological Satellites, an intergovernmental organisation created through an international convention agreed by 18 European Member States.

World Meteorological Organization (www.wmo.int)

The United Nation's Agency for Weather, this site provides information about international research projects, technical co-operation between nations, WMO's education and training activities and links to meteorological sites around the world. The International Cloud Atlas (www.wmocloudatlas.org), first published in the late nineteenth century, is now available online. This online version was relaunched in March 2017 and includes new cloud classifications such as volutes and asperitas.

National Aeronautics Space Association (www.nasa.gov)

NASA is an agency of the United States Government, responsible for that nation's public space program. The website has a wealth of information about international space stations, planets, space technology and data from space satellites.

UM Weather (http://cirrus.sprl.umich.edu/wxnet)

This site provides access to thousands of meteorological sites around the world, from which weather maps, weather forecasts, climatological information, climatic data, radar images, satellite images, and software can be obtained.

UK Weather Shop

(www.weathershop.co.uk) This shop sells books, traditional and electronic instruments, educational material, software for downloading data from a weather station and much more.

Meteorologica (www.meteorologica.co.uk)

A weather superstore that sells books, meteorological instruments, weather software, wireless weather stations, webcams and much more.

Acknowledgements

The Royal Meteorological Society would like to thank the following: Bob Riddaway, Geoff Jenkins, Storm Dunlop, Met Office, BBC, Samantha Hall, Guinness World Records

Picture acknowledgements

© Elissa Nesheim: cover, pp. 2, 15, 22, 32, 42, 54, 64, 76, 86, 96, 108, 118, 130, 140, 170; © Shutterstock/one AND only: cover spine artwork; © R. K. Pilsbury FRPS (Royal Meteorological Society Collection): p. 14, (cirrus, cirrostratus, cirrocumulus, contrails), p.15, (castellanus) p. 16 (stratocumulus, stratus, fractostratus, nimbostratus); © Malcolm Walker: p.14 (uncinus), p.15 (altostratus, undulates, other altocumulus), p. 16 (cumulus, cumulonimbus); © Jacob Kollegger: p. 15 (lenticular); © Shutterstock/Reamolko: weather icons; © Shutterstock/Magic Pencil: weather icons watercolour artwork; © Shutterstock/Asymme3: headings watercolour artwork; © Shutterstock/SkillUp: graph paper

Brimming with creative inspiration, how-to projects and useful information to enrich your everyday life, Quarto Knows is a favourite destination for those pursuing their interests and passions. Visit our site and dig deeper with our books into your area of interest: Quarto Creates, Quarto Cooks, Quarto Homes, Quarto Lives, Quarto Drives, Quarto Explores, Quarto Gifts, or Quarto Kids.

Weather Watcher's 3-Year Log Book

© 2017 Quarto Publishing plc. Text © Royal Meteorolgical Society 2017. Illustrations © as listed above.

First Published in 2007. This edition published in 2017 by Frances Lincoln, an imprint of The Quarto Group. The Old Brewery, 6 Blundell Street, London N7 9BH, United Kingdom.
www.QuartoKnows.com

All rights reserved.
No part of this publication may be reproduced, stored in a retrieval system, or transmitted, in any form, or by any means, electronic, mechanical, photocopying, recording or otherwise without the prior written permission of the publisher or a licence permitting restricted copying. In the United Kingdom such licences are issued by the Copyright Licensing Agency, Barnard's Inn, 86 Fetter Lane, London, EC4A 1EN

A catalogue record for this book is available from the British Library.

ISBN 978 0 7112 3912 8

Printed and bound in China

1 2 3 4 5 6 7 8 9